TRANSACTIONS OF THE

AMERICAN PHILOSOPHICAL SOCIETY

· HELD AT PHILADELPHIA

FOR PROMOTING USEFUL KNOWLEDGE

VOLUME 72, PART 1 · 1982

Franklin the Diplomat: the French Mission

JONATHAN R. DULL

THE AMERICAN PHILOSOPHICAL SOCIETY

INDEPENDENCE SQUARE: PHILADELPHIA

1982

Library of Congress Catalog
Card Number 81-68191
International Standard Book Number 0-87169-721-1
US ISSN 0065-9746

To Veronica and Robert

CONTENTS

	Page
Preface	vii
Abbreviations	ix
I. Franklin's diplomatic background	1
II. The development of Franklin's negotiating style	11
III. Franklin the negotiator: securing the alliance	19
IV. Franklin as head of mission	33
V. Franklin and the functioning of the alliance	43
VI. Franklin the negotiator: securing the peace	53
VII. Franklin: diplomat and man	65
Index	73

PREFACE

Within the last few years there have been numerous breakthroughs in our understanding of Benjamin Franklin. New studies have given a more balanced and sophisticated picture of Franklin the religious thinker, Franklin the politician, and Franklin the family man.[1] While we also have a superb study of his diplomatic thought,[2] there as yet has been no modern study of Franklin as a practicing diplomat. The material for such a work is available; photocopies of all his correspondence from France have been collected at Yale University as part of the enormous Franklin Papers editorial project.[3] A full treatment of his day-to-day activities in France, however, would take many years of research. My purposes are more modest: to look at how he approached his job as a diplomat and to evaluate his performance.[4] I will restrict myself to the wartime years of his French mission and concentrate on the activities I consider most important; to illuminate Franklin I will discuss the individual people with whom he worked, the polity he represented, and the society in which he lived.

In one sense this book is an individual effort, in another sense a collective one. Since July 1977 I have been a member of the editorial staff of the Papers of Benjamin Franklin, working during regular hours on volumes

---

[1] Melvin H. Buxbaum, *Benjamin Franklin and the Zealous Presbyterians* (University Park: The Pennsylvania State University Press, 1975); James H. Hutson, *Pennsylvania Politics, 1746–1770: The Movement for Royal Government and Its Consequences* (Princeton: Princeton University Press, 1972); Claude-Anne Lopez and Eugenia W. Herbert, *The Private Franklin: The Man and His Family* (New York: W. W. Norton and Company, 1975).

[2] Gerald Stourzh, *Benjamin Franklin and American Foreign Policy*, 2d ed. (Chicago: University of Chicago Press, 1969).

[3] For a description of the Franklin Papers collection see Leonard W. Labaree, "In Search of B. Franklin," *The William and Mary Quarterly*, 3rd ser. 16 (1959): 188–97; and Leonard W. Labaree and Whitfield J. Bell, Jr., "The Papers of Benjamin Franklin: A Progress Report," *Proceedings of The American Philosophical Society* 101 (1957): 532–34. Labaree edited the first fourteen volumes of *The Papers of Benjamin Franklin* (New Haven and London: Yale University Press, 1959 —); the subsequent eight volumes have been edited by William B. Willcox. The total project will comprise at least fifty volumes. The number of secondary sources for Franklin's mission is enormous; an annotated guide to books and articles relating to Franklin is currently in progress under the editorship of Melvin H. Buxbaum. Publication of the first volume is expected shortly. For a bibliography of the Franco-American alliance see Jonathan R. Dull, *The French Navy and American Independence: A Study of Arms and Diplomacy, 1774–1787* (Princeton: Princeton University Press, 1975), pp. 396–423 and Jonathan R. Dull, "American Foreign Relations before the Constitution: A Historiographical Wasteland" in *American Foreign Relations: A Historiographical Review*, Gerald K. Haines and J. Samuel Walker, eds. (Westport, Conn.: Greenwood Press, 1981), pp. 3–15.

[4] The word "diplomat" is an anachronism in terms of Franklin's century: see William James Roosen, *The Age of Louis XIV: The Rise of Modern Diplomacy* (Cambridge, Mass.: Schenkman Publishing Company, 1976), p. 6. Unfortunately, the more accurate title of minister presents possibilities of confusion for modern readers—rather hilarious possibilities in conjunction with Franklin. Franklin assuredly was not an ambassador, which in his time carried connotations of nobility.

22 and 23 of Franklin's correspondence and during my off-hours on *Franklin the Diplomat*. The judgments and opinions expressed in this book are my own; what understanding of Franklin it contains, however, is so much a product of my interaction with my colleagues that I can hardly claim it as entirely mine. I extend my thanks therefore to my colleagues and friends Bill Willcox, Doug Arnold, Dorothy Bridgwater, Claude Lopez, and Kitty Prelinger. A special thanks goes to our chief editor, Bill Willcox, who extended permission to use for my purposes the thousands of folders of photocopies of Franklin documents upon which this book is based.

ABBREVIATIONS

AAE	Archives du Ministère des Affaires Étrangères, Paris
AHN	Archivo Histórico Nacional, Madrid
APS	American Philosophical Society, Philadelphia
APS-Bache	American Philosophical Society: Bache Collection
Ct	Connecticut State Library, Hartford
CtHi	Connecticut Historical Society, Hartford
CtY	Yale University Library, New Haven
DLC	Library of Congress, Washington
DNA	National Archives, Washington
MdAn	United States Naval Academy, Annapolis
MH	Harvard University Library, Cambridge, Mass.
MHi	Massachusetts Historical Society, Boston
MiU-C	William L. Clements Library, University of Michigan, Ann Arbor
NHi	New-York Historical Society, New York City
NjP	Princeton University Library, Princeton, N.J.
NN	New York Public Library, New York City
NNC	Columbia University Library, New York City
PHi	Historical Society of Pennsylvania, Philadelphia
PRO	Public Record Office, London
PU	University of Pennsylvania Library, Philadelphia
ScHi	South Carolina Historical Society, Charleston
ViU	University of Virginia Library, Charlottesville

TRANS. AMER. PHIL. SOC.
VOL. 72 PT. 1, 1982

I. FRANKLIN'S DIPLOMATIC BACKGROUND

If George Washington is the Zeus in America's pantheon, then Benjamin Franklin is our Proteus. None of the other founding fathers is as difficult to categorize; no other career assumed so many forms. Publisher, author, politician, scientist, colonial lobbyist in London and finally, at the age of seventy, diplomat, Franklin's is the archetypal story of the American capable of performing any task. His mission to Paris is not only the first but the most enduring success story in American diplomacy. To tell the story realistically is not easy, since even the beginning of his mission has an almost mythic quality: the frail, elderly man and his two grandchildren being rowed from an American warship to a French fishing village. What prepared him for so heroic a role?

To answer the question it is necessary to begin not with Franklin the diplomat but with Franklin the man. The Franklin who arrived in France was the product of the experiences of an extraordinarily varied life and in a real sense all of it was of use to him as a diplomat—the practicality of Franklin the printer, the eloquence of Franklin the writer, the skill in discussion of Franklin the politician, the rationality of Franklin the scientist. It would be redundant to attempt to summarize all of his prior life. We have his autobiography and a modern edition of his papers; moreover, his attitudes and experiences have been more thoroughly studied than those of virtually any other American of his century.[1] However, a few reflections on the specific ways those experiences prepared him for his mission to France may be useful.

The most relevant of these episodes were his two "missions" to England as colonial agent for the Pennsylvania Assembly. After making his fortune as a printer he had retired at the age of forty-one in 1748 to devote his life to science and to public affairs. A member of the Pennsylvania Assembly since 1751, he was selected in 1757 to resolve its disagreements with the Penn family, proprietors of the colony.[2] The Franklin who traveled to London to meet Thomas and Richard Penn was a far different person from the more experienced and realistic Franklin who sailed from Philadelphia for France nineteen years later. There were seeds of the latter Franklin already present in 1757, however. The prior events of his life had already shown a number of characteristics which, deepened in England, would form the

---

[1] Those wishing a general introduction to Franklin's life should consult the entry in the *Dictionary of American Biography* and the Franklin chronology in Leonard W. Labaree, ed., *The Autobiography of Benjamin Franklin* (New Haven and London: Yale University Press, 1964), pp. 303-22.

[2] James H. Hutson, *Pennsylvania Politics, 1746–1770: The Movement for Royal Government and Its Consequences* (Princeton: Princeton University Press, 1972), pp. 33–41.

core of Franklin the diplomat. They included a remarkable flexibility of mind, a negotiator's temperament, and an extraordinary breadth of vision.

The first of these traits, the suppleness and power of Franklin's mind, defies simple explanation. Paul Conner, in the best treatment of that mind, has shown the order underlying its freedom and has suggested some of the sources of its order—the years of working with racks of printer's type, the exposure to the structure of eighteenth-century science, the social experience of living and succeeding in the most orderly (yet socially and intellectually open) of American cities.[3] The second of these traits, a temperament adapted to negotiation, is barely more explainable. Franklin's extraordinary social and financial success in Philadelphia was only in part attributable to his business acumen and writing skills. He lacked the financial capital and family background necessary to promise success even in Philadelphia; his capacity for making friends and for tapping the energy and talents (and financial resources) of others was indispensable to his advancement. As a politician, too, he prospered by his persuasiveness. By inclination he was a conciliator, a seeker of consensus—invaluable traits in conducting an alliance with a French court whose interests often differed from his countrymen's. Ultimately, however, Franklin's temperament also is unfathomable. How did he escape the straitjacket of eighteenth-century religion? Where did he derive his ability to befriend people of all ages and social backgrounds? These questions are unanswerable, although surely his own humble background, his years in England, his travels in America as deputy postmaster general, and his scientific correspondence helped preserve him from provincialism and rigidity.[4]

The third of his traits, the breadth of his vision, is easier to explain. Gerald Stourzh has shown how the great war with France of 1754–63 focused Franklin's concern on America's growth and external security. This concern drew him beyond Pennsylvania toward a vision of British America as central to the power and prosperity of the British Empire.[5] His subsequent disillusionment with Britain would deepen his commitment not only to Pennsylvania but to British North America as a whole.

Franklin arrived in England as the representative of the Pennsylvania Assembly to negotiate directly with the proprietors rather than through the proprietors' appointed governor in Philadelphia. Such negotiations were not really much different from those with which Franklin was familiar. When his efforts were met with contempt, however, Franklin's role changed. Gradually he became the equivalent of a lobbyist, using the Lon-

---

[3] Paul W. Conner, *Poor Richard's Politicks: Benjamin Franklin and the New American Order* (New York: Oxford University Press, 1966), pp. 13, 173–217. However, Conner has slighted the contribution of a generous, loyal, and supportive wife to the underlying order of Franklin's life.

[4] Franklin lived in London as an apprentice printer from 1724–1726, besides his stays as Pennsylvania representative described below. He served as deputy postmaster general of North America from 1753 to 1774. His international reputation as a scientist dates from 1751, when his experiments on electricity were first published.

[5] Gerald Stourzh, *Benjamin Franklin and American Foreign Policy*, 2d ed. (Chicago: University of Chicago Press, 1969), pp. 33–112.

don newspapers and his contacts in Parliament for his political objectives. His mission largely was a failure; he returned to Pennsylvania in 1762 with an animus against the Penns and a desire to replace proprietary government with direct government by the king. Two years later he returned to England on the assembly's behalf, still pursuing the chimera of royal government.[6]

Soon, however, the focus of Franklin's activities shifted. The most important event in producing that shift was the Stamp Act crisis. At first willing to nominate a friend as stamp distributor for Pennsylvania, he soon learned that both principle and prudence lay in opposition to the legislation.[7] His testimony to the House of Commons on behalf of its repeal[8] established his reputation as a spokesman for American interests. In 1768 he became the agent in England of Georgia, in 1769 of the New Jersey House of Representatives, in 1770 of the Massachusetts House of Representatives. Franklin's attitude toward the empire evolved as his responsibilities brought him into close contact with British governing circles. Along with his hopes for royal government for Pennsylvania, he had wanted to win consent for a plan whereby the British government would loan money to the colonies and use the interest for revenue. This would aid colonial development while preserving the colonies' right to levy their own taxes.[9] By mid-1767 his hopes here too had been extinguished.[10] A final burst of optimism about royal government rose and flickered in 1768, but old battles by then were becoming irrelevant.[11] Franklin found a new crusade, which was equally futile but far grander in scope: to increase and strengthen the party in England in favor of America "by every effort of Tongue and Pen."[12] He contributed to his own defeat, however, by leaking to his friends the letters of Governor Hutchinson of Massachusetts, an opponent of conciliation. Humiliated publicly before the Privy Council as a result, Franklin lost his effectiveness as a spokesman for conciliation.[13] He remained in England long enough, however, to make one last attempt to prevent a

---

[6] Hutson, *Pennsylvania Politics*, pp. 33–69, 122–46, 178–83, 205–07.

[7] Ibid., p. 190; Benjamin H. Newcomb, *Franklin and Galloway: A Political Partnership* (New Haven and London: Yale University Press, 1972), pp. 113–14, 126–28; Edmund S. Morgan and Helen N. Morgan, *The Stamp Act Crisis: Prologue to Rebellion* (Chapel Hill: The University of North Carolina Press, 1953), pp. 238–57.

[8] Leonard W. Labaree, ed., *Papers of Benjamin Franklin* (New Haven and London: Yale University Press, 1959–), 13: 124–62.

[9] Newcomb, *Franklin and Galloway*, pp. 110–12; Labaree, *Papers of Benjamin Franklin*, 12: 47–60; E. James Ferguson, *The Power of the Purse: A History of American Public Finance, 1776–1790* (Chapel Hill: The University of North Carolina Press, 1961), pp. 19–20.

[10] See Franklin to Joseph Galloway, 13 June 1767, Labaree, *Papers of Benjamin Franklin*, 14: 180–85.

[11] One such battle was Franklin's long struggle against the "Presbyterians" described in Melvin H. Buxbaum, *Benjamin Franklin and the Zealous Presbyterians* (University Park: The Pennsylvania State University Press, 1975).

[12] Franklin to Joseph Galloway, 20 August 1768, Willcox, *Papers of Benjamin Franklin*, 15: 189–90.

[13] Jack M. Soisin, *Agents and Merchants: British Colonial Policy and the Origins of the American Revolution, 1763–1775* (Lincoln: University of Nebraska Press, 1965), p. 161. Conversely, Franklin's credibility was more firmly established among Americans. Compare Arthur Lee's letter to Sam Adams of 10 June 1771 with that of 8 February 1774, Richard Henry Lee, ed., *Life of Arthur Lee, LL.D.*, 2 vols. (Boston: Wells and Lilly, 1829), 1: 215–18, 240–42.

rupture between Britain and America. Contacted through two prominent London Quakers, he negotiated for several months during the winter of 1774–1775 with members of the cabinet.[14] The only certainty about these shadowy negotiations is their hopelessness. After the Boston Tea Party and Coercive Acts no grounds remained for compromise, and only Franklin's departure from England prevented his arrest.[15] His second mission, like his first, had ended in failure.

What had Franklin acquired from his experience? Obviously his loyalties shifted away from Britain, but surely this would have happened had he remained in America. He did learn at first hand the "corruption" of British politics and society and the mean-spiritedness and inflexibility of the North government. Most important, however, in the development of Franklin as a diplomat may have been his experience at court. Franklin never lost a certain awe for royalty (George III excepted), but by the time he reached France he was much less impressed by titles than was someone like John Adams. Moreover, in comparison to Adams, Franklin, in spite of his rather considerable vanity, proved impervious to flattery—and equally impervious to intimidation. The years of frustration at the hands of the great of England at least helped teach him realism and toughen his character. He also learned the manners of court society, a vital acquisition given the importance of reassuring the French nobility that American revolutionaries posed no threat to them. John Adams admitted Franklin's gifts:

Who, in the name of astonishment, in all America, at that time had a knowledge of courts? Franklin alone had resided in England as a despised and scorned agent at the Court of St. James's. In address and good breeding, he was excelled by very few Americans. In France and in Holland, where he lived with me, I know that his manners, address, learning, knowledge, and good sense were acknowledged by all who conversed with him. If by "address" you mean graceful attitudes and elegant motions and gestures, he had received as genteel an education as any man in America; if you mean a civil and polite conversation, he was, at least, equal to any American then in Europe.[16]

One suspects that Franklin also learned another valuable lesson. While in France, he managed to avoid one of the most common failings of diplomats, that of trying to influence a policymaker through his subordinates. Sir James Harris, one of the most clever diplomats of the period, blighted his mission to St. Petersburg by not realizing that Catherine the Great made her own policy decisions.[17] Thomas Jefferson as Franklin's successor assigned undue weight to the influence of the French foreign min-

---

[14] Willcox, *Papers of Benjamin Franklin*, 21: 360–65 and following.

[15] Ibid., 21: xxxv. Legal action had been brought against Franklin by the brother of one of Hutchinson's correspondents.

[16] John Adams to Mercy Warren, 8 August 1807, *Collections of the Massachusetts Historical Society*, 5th ser. (1878) 4: 446.

[17] Isabel de Madariaga, *Britain, Russia and the Armed Neutrality of 1780: Sir James Harris's Mission to St. Petersburg during the American Revolution* (New Haven and London: Yale University Press, 1962).

ister's undersecretaries.[18] As a lobbyist in England Franklin had used subordinates to gain access to the powerful,[19] and in the end it availed him
nothing. One of the causes of his later success in France was his dealing
directly and exclusively with the French foreign minister or with those
designated by him. Franklin's rigorous avoidance of intrigue could hardly
have been unrelated to the lessons taught by the English court.

Much of the practical experience he gained in England proved of little
relevance to his French mission. Because of the different political and social
circumstances he found little or no use for many of his familiar tactics—
the use of the merchant community for lobbying, the writing of newspaper
articles, the cultivating of legislators. What he carried with him to France
were the qualities of character fostered by his English missions—patience,
tact, prudence.

In early May 1775 he returned to Philadelphia to learn of the recent
battles of Lexington and Concord and to be appointed to the Second Continental Congress by the Pennsylvania Assembly. During the next eighteen
months the septuagenarian Franklin was selected for thirty-four congressional committees and for the position of postmaster general, while he was
also elected president of the Pennsylvania Committee of Safety and president of the Pennsylvania Constitutional Convention. He furthermore was
elected but did not serve as an Indian commissioner, as a member of the
Philadelphia Committee of Inspection and Observation, and as a member
of the Pennsylvania Assembly.[20] In the service of the congress he traveled
to Cambridge to draft regulations for the American army, to Montreal in
an attempt to salvage relations with the Canadians, and to Staten Island
to negotiate with Admiral Richard Howe, British peace commissioner. During these months he was connected with virtually every aspect of American
and Pennsylvania political life from the defense of the Delaware River to
the drafting of the Declaration of Independence.[21] Franklin's final honor
was to be selected by Congress on 26 September 1776 as one of its three
commissioners to the court of France; a month later he sailed for Europe.

Franklin's service as a congressman gives eloquent testimony to the
breadth of his interests, to the flexibility of his mind, and to his dedication
to public service. He later told Arthur Lee he had worked twelve hours a
day on public business.[22] John Adams complained that Franklin had con-

---

[18] Thomas Jefferson to James Madison, 30 January 1787, Julian P. Boyd, ed., *The Papers of Thomas Jefferson*, 19 vols. to date (Princeton: Princeton University Press, 1950–), 11: 96.

[19] Michael G. Kammen, *A Rope of Sand: The Colonial Agents and the American Revolution* (Ithaca: Cornell University Press, 1968), pp. 69–70.

[20] Willcox, *Papers of Benjamin Franklin*, 22: pp. xlviii–lii. Franklin turned seventy in January 1776.

[21] For Franklin and Pennsylvania politics see Richard A. Ryerson, *"The Revolution is now begun": The Radical Committees of Philadelphia, 1765–1776* (Philadelphia: University of Pennsylvania Press, 1978), which reduces Franklin's role to reasonable proportions. Also useful is David Hawke, *In the Midst of a Revolution* (Philadelphia: University of Pennsylvania Press, 1961).

[22] R. H. Lee, *Life of Arthur Lee*, 1: 343–46; this extract from Arthur Lee's journal contains Franklin's description of the obstacles faced by Congress and the inspired improvisation with which Congress met them. For details of Franklin's daily schedule see Franklin's letters of 7

tributed little to debate, during which he often fell asleep;[23] little wonder. True, most of his congressional committees were not standing committees and thus disappeared when their task was finished. True also that much of his participation in Pennsylvania politics was only nominal. Nevertheless, the range of his activities raises questions about his priorities. Is there a unifying theme to Franklin's set of services?

Obviously no single heading can encompass all of Franklin's activities and interests. One issue, however, does appear repeatedly: the relationship of America to the outside world. Two of his most important public papers, the "Resolution on Trade" and the "Intended Vindication and Offer," his letters to friends in England, his meeting with Howe, his participation in the drafting of the Declaration of Independence—all represent attempts to assign Britain the responsibility for breaking "that fine and noble China Vase the British Empire."[24] His mission to Montreal was prompted by the breakdown of relations between the Continental Army and the Canadians whose loyalty Congress still hoped to win. His active membership for several months on the Secret Committee (later called the Committee of Commerce) was concerned with finding sources of munitions and clothing outside America. It is arguable that his most important committee assignment, however, was on the Committee of Secret Correspondence, established 29 November 1775 "for the sole purpose of corresponding with our friends in Great Britain, Ireland and other parts of the world."[25] The committee's foreign correspondents initially were comprised of Franklin's own contacts. Indeed, it is hard to distinguish between his personal and official correspondence since on occasion he was asked by the committee to write his friends on its behalf. It was he who drafted the instructions for Silas Deane, who in March 1776 departed for France as the committee's representative.[26] When news arrived six months later that the French government was willing secretly to aid the revolution, it came in a letter addressed to Franklin.[27] He therefore was a natural choice to join Deane and Arthur Lee, a former colonial agent in London, when Congress decided as a result to establish a formal mission in France.

Franklin's service in Congress in many ways was the culmination of his diplomatic education and the key to his subsequent effectiveness in France.

July 1775 to Joseph Priestley and Jonathan Shipley, Willcox, *Papers of Benjamin Franklin*, 22: 92–93, 94.

[23] L. H. Butterfield, ed., *Diary and Autobiography of John Adams*, 4 vols. (Cambridge: The Belknap Press of Harvard University Press, 1961), 4: 337–38.

[24] Willcox, *Papers of Benjamin Franklin*, 22: 91–98, 112–20, 126–28, 485–86, 591–93. The quotation is from Franklin to Lord Richard Howe, 20 July 1776, ibid., p. 520.

[25] Worthington Chauncey Ford et al., eds., *Journals of the Continental Congress, 1774–1789*, 35 vols. (Washington: Library of Congress and National Archives, 1904–1976), 3: 392.

[26] Deane was already planning to go to Europe as representative of a trading consortium dealing with the Secret Committee; his mission thus was half public and half private. See Willcox, *Papers of Benjamin Franklin*, 22: 369–74. Arthur Lee and C. G. F. Dumas merely had intelligence gathering functions.

[27] Jacques Barbeu-Dubourg to Franklin, 10 June–2 July 1776, Willcox, *Papers of Benjamin Franklin*, 22: 453–71.

Franklin's post in France was a political appointment; for him to keep it for eight and a half years became one of his greatest political accomplishments. Partly this achievement was a result of his performance in France, but one suspects it was even more dependent on his prior performance in Congress. While in Philadelphia he established friendships with members of every faction, from moderates like Robert Morris and John Jay to radicals like John Adams. His care not to be tied to a single faction was the key to his political longevity, since it made it difficult for an opposition to coalesce against him.[28] His word, moreover, generally was trusted in Congress because of his proven record. His service in Congress not only secured a political base in Philadelphia; it underlay his effectiveness with the French government. As well as any politician who ever lived, he understood the politician's dependence on his constituents. Franklin as diplomat took enormous care not to go beyond his instructions (or more accurately not to be caught going beyond his instructions); his chief imprudence was in not corresponding with Congress more frequently. His knowledge of his constituents' wishes and his faithfulness to them meant that his word could be trusted at the French court at Versailles as it was in Philadelphia. When he spoke about Congress, about the American people or about the American army, his was the voice of experience. His optimism about the future of the American cause was persuasive because his opinion could be counted upon to be realistic. Given the differences between the world views of an aristocratic French foreign minister and the American commissioners, the need for establishing trust was vital. It took all the openness, experience, and realism of a Franklin to interpret the needs and wishes of American revolutionaries to the French court and vice versa. Such a task could not have been accomplished by someone of less experience (like Silas Deane) or someone too closely linked with the radical faction in Congress (like John Adams).[29]

Although Franklin's background for diplomacy was unparalleled in America, there is a danger of overestimating his qualifications. Certainly his experience (like that of Washington) had molded and strengthened his character and deepened his self-confidence, but like Washington his professional preparation contained gaps. These gaps Franklin would have to fill on his own. (In one sense Franklin was worse off than Washington; neither man possessed a mentor, but Washington at least could tap the experience of professional soldiers like Charles Lee and Horatio Gates while mastering

---

[28] See Conrad-Alexandre Gérard, French minister to the United States, to Vergennes, 11 July 1779, John J. Meng, ed., *Dispatches and Instructions of Conrad Alexander Gérard, 1778-1780* (Baltimore: The Johns Hopkins University Press, 1939), p. 795. This pattern of working with men he liked and attempting to stay out of factional disputes also characterized Franklin's political views when first elected to the Pennsylvania Assembly. William S. Hanna, *Benjamin Franklin and Pennsylvania Politics* (Stanford: Stanford University Press, 1964) pp. 48-53.

[29] The radical or "Eastern" party in Congress was regarded by the French as hostile to the alliance. For Vergennes's distrust of John Adams because of his connection with the "Eastern" party see James H. Hutson, *John Adams and the Diplomacy of the American Revolution* (Lexington: The University Press of Kentucky, 1980) p. 57.

his craft.) The mission to France would test Franklin's knowledge of economics, military affairs, law and European statecraft; his background in each included serious flaws.

Of these areas Franklin's background was strongest in economics. From his service on the Secret Committee and the Pennsylvania Committee of Safety he had learned about the needs of the American army and the functioning of a wartime economy. He had seen most sections of the country on his postal tours and had lobbied in London for colonies from Massachusetts to Georgia. He had, moreover, not only a wide knowledge of the American economy but a splendid grounding in the most advanced economic thought of his day. Perhaps most important, Franklin was a sophisticated and consistent advocate of free trade—an enormously useful set of beliefs, since the fundamental premise of the Franco-American alliance was that American independence would mean France could take from Britain a major share of American trade.[30] Nevertheless Franklin himself was the first to admit the deficiencies in his economic education. One of his most frequent complaints was his lack of understanding of the commercial matters with which he constantly had to deal until the arrival of an American consul in 1782. Although such complaints were a reaction to the time and trouble demanded by commercial matters, one should not question Franklin's sincerity. In spite of his excellent business sense,[31] he did not have a merchant's firsthand commercial knowledge. It took almost a year after the signing of the Treaty of Commerce for Franklin and his fellow commissioners to make inquiries about which nations held most favored nation status in France and what duties they paid.[32] In spite of his desire to stimulate trade and aid American merchants in France, he lacked the mercantile experience to do an adequate job.

He also lacked the background to contribute to the making of military strategy. To be sure, he was not totally lacking in experience; in addition to his congressional contacts with the Continental Army, he had helped

[30] See "Memorandum for Rayneval to give to Vergennes," 6 July 1778 (AAE). For identification of manuscript repositories, see Abbreviations, p. ix. I have consulted photocopies of these documents at the Franklin Papers editorial office, Yale University. Many of the documents cited in manuscript have been published in such documentary collections as Francis P. Wharton, ed., *The Revolutionary Diplomatic Correspondence of the United States*, 6 vols. (Washington: Government Printing Office, 1889), Albert Henry Smyth, ed., *The Writings of Benjamin Franklin*, 10 vols. (New York: The Macmillan Company, 1907), and Edward E. Hale and Edward E. Hale, Jr., eds., *Franklin in France*, 2 vols. (Boston: Roberts Brothers, 1887–1888). Also of use are the microfilm edition of *Benjamin Franklin's Account Books* produced by Scholarly Resources Publications and the American Philosophical Society and two calendars of Franklin papers: I. Minis Hays, ed., *Calendar of the Papers of Benjamin Franklin in the Library of the American Philosophical Society*, 5 vols. (Philadelphia: American Philosophical Society, 1908) and Worthington Chauncey Ford, ed., *List of the Benjamin Franklin Papers in the Library of Congress* (Washington: Government Printing Office, 1908).

[31] See for example his letter to Jonathan Williams, Jr., of 19 March 1779 (DLC), in which he skillfully dissects Arthur Lee's ignorance of accounting procedures.

[32] American Commissioners to John Lloyd et al., 26 January 1779 (DLC); Benjamin Franklin to Joshua Johnson, 17 March 1779 (DLC).

organize the Philadelphia militia in 1747, and in 1756 had briefly commanded the defense of Northampton County, Pennsylvania.[33] When called on for advice, his opinions generally were sound, such as his recommendation against a plan to rescue American prisoners which did not take account of the need for a rendezvous point for the rescue party.[34] Franklin's advice was seldom asked, however, and seldom volunteered. The American war as seen from Europe chiefly was a naval war. America had no navy of which to speak, and neither Franklin nor any other American had any experience in serious naval operations. Franklin had no pretensions, as had John Adams, to knowledge in the field and he had the common sense not to annoy the French.[35] On the other hand, his ability to argue for the allocation of French military resources to the American theater of war was severely circumscribed because he was not regarded as possessing military experience or knowledge. Fortunately, Lafayette spent part of the war in France. From necessity (as well as by choice) Franklin compensated by using him as his voice on military matters.

Two subjects of which Franklin was almost totally ignorant were international law and commercial law.[36] This did not pose major problems because he could obtain expert advice when needed. Far more serious was his ignorance of the interests, needs, and views of the various European states, including France. No American diplomat of the period had the slightest knowledge of what we would call geopolitics; on this subject Arthur Lee's dispatches were consistently wrongheaded, Adams's trite, and Franklin's silent. Franklin was willing to learn but there were no objective teachers; the comte de Vergennes, the French foreign minister, hardly could be expected to reveal the rationale of his policy. Although, as we shall see, the American's ignorance was highly dangerous,[37] in one critical sense it proved highly advantageous. Franklin and his colleagues had no idea that Vergennes's major diplomatic concern was France's declining position in the European balance of power, particularly in relation to Austria and Russia. Franklin, though, did share a common language with Vergennes; both were men who profoundly hated war but were willing to fight in the interests of national security. Franklin grasped that Vergennes's goal was that of weakening Britain, but did not understand that the underlying

---

[33] A brief survey of Franklin's military career is found in James Bennett Nolan, *General Benjamin Franklin: The Military Career of a Philosopher* (Philadelphia: University of Pennsylvania Press, 1936).

[34] Franklin to the marquis de Lafayette, 28 March 1782 (DLC).

[35] Adam's statements on naval affairs range from jejune to the idiotic; examples include John Adams to William Carmichael, 12 May 1780, Wharton, *Revolutionary Diplomatic Correspondence*, 3: 672–73; John Adams to Richard Cranch, 17 December 1781, L. H. Butterfield and Marc Friedlander, eds., *Adams Family Correspondence*, 4 vols. to date (Cambridge: The Belknap Press of Harvard University Press, 1963–), 4: 267. One of Franklin's few comments on naval affairs is in R. H. Lee, *Life of Arthur Lee*, 1: 405.

[36] Conner, *Poor Richard's Politicks*, p. 276 points out that law was the subject in which Franklin had the least interest.

[37] Particularly during the peace negotiations of 1782; see below, chapter VI.

reason was to permit France to cope with the powers of eastern Europe.[38] Repeatedly Franklin argued that American independence would do precisely what Vergennes hoped: by reducing British trade it would undercut the basis of British commercial and naval power.[39] Ironically, Franklin was reinforcing a totally false preconception. The loss of her monopoly over American trade in the long run did not weaken Britain. American merchants continued to trade with their British counterparts, and within a few years Britain virtually drove France out of the American market. The French government was bankrupted for a policy which brought it no real benefits.

There are those that fortune asks to be the recipient of her smiles. Franklin was such a one, and if this too is beyond historical analysis we at least can say he had the wisdom not to refuse the favor. He was the beneficiary of the historical accident that France for her own reasons wished for exactly the same thing as did America: a sovereign and independent United States free of any British presence. As Gerald Stourzh points out, Franklin finally found in Vergennes someone who would respond to his appeals to reciprocity and mutual self-interest.[40] To draw maximum benefit from the happy accident of this shared interest, Franklin would have to find the best approach; in the next chapter we will examine the development of his style of negotiation.

---

[38] I have discussed French foreign policy at length in Jonathan R. Dull, *French Navy and American Independence: A Study of Arms and Diplomacy, 1774–1787* (Princeton: Princeton University Press, 1975), and more succinctly in "France and the American Revolution Seen as Tragedy" in Ronald T. Hoffman and Peter J. Albert eds., *Diplomacy and Revolution: The Franco-American Alliance of 1778* (Charlottesville: The University Press of Virginia, 1981), pp. 73–106.

[39] See for example Franklin's first memoir to Vergennes, 5 January 1777, Benjamin Franklin Stevens, ed., *Facsimiles of Manuscripts in European Archives Relating to America, 1775–1783*, 25 vols. (London: privately printed, 1889–1898), 6: no. 614.

[40] Stourzh, *Benjamin Franklin and American Foreign Policy*, pp. 148, 253.

II. THE DEVELOPMENT OF FRANKLIN'S NEGOTIATING STYLE

Before 1776 Franklin had failed in negotiation after negotiation—to gain greater autonomy from the Penns, to obtain royal government, to win approval for land grants in the Ohio valley for the Walpole Company in which he had invested, and finally to resolve the Anglo-American crisis of 1774–1775. His record in France presents an amazing contrast—treaties of alliance and commerce largely on America's own terms, some 40,000,000 livres of French financial aid (equivalent to about $80,-000,000 in contemporary purchasing power), and finally peace terms with Britain which left an experienced diplomat like Vergennes awed. Franklin may well have grown in toughness, shrewdness, and eloquence, but such a change in fortune demands more of an explanation. Obviously the major difference is that possibilities for consensus existed in France which did not in England. I suspect, though, that there was another factor involved. While he was in France, Franklin perfected a style of negotiation beautifully adapted to the requirements of America's situation. As we shall see, he defined this style and though his definition sounds quaint, it perfectly describes his negotiating tactics. Franklin's approach to negotiation was to play the courted virgin.[1]

This style of calculated passivity represents a contrast not only to the compulsive activity of a John Adams but also to Franklin's own techniques as a London lobbyist. His fifteen years in England had been devoted in large part to winning the support of the great, a life spent in antechambers. One of the constants in his personality, so often commented upon as to be now a cliché, was his hatred of being dependent. Those years as a colonial agent must have been painful indeed for the poor boy become world-famed scientist, now again dependent on others. I suspect that what caused Franklin to change his approach was the demonstration that all his reasonableness and accommodation brought only contempt. All the years of trying to win friends for America resulted only in his humiliation before the Privy Council. In a functioning republic like Pennsylvania one could trade, compromise, and accommodate differences, but in a corrupt court society (as Franklin viewed Britain) only strength counted.

The negotiations with the British government during the winter of 1774–1775 reveal a new approach to negotiation by Franklin. Not until he reached France did he develop the tools to turn weakness into strength, but by late

---

[1] Franklin's comparing himself to a courted virgin will be quoted below. For his adopting a related political style (which Conner calls the strategy of humility) see Paul W. Conner, *Poor Richard's Politicks: Benjamin Franklin and the New American Order* (New York: Oxford University Press, 1966), p. 156.

1774 he had learned to avoid making grandiose proposals. Franklin's negotiating posture became more cautious and reserved. He was willing only to propose hints concerning the terms which might produce a durable Anglo-American union.[2] Cautious indeed; even the entry of Lord Howe into the negotiations failed to seduce Franklin into concessions for which he had no authority.[3] The negotiations never stood a chance, but Franklin could have destroyed himself politically in America by pursuing phantoms; he had acquired the self-control to avoid doing so.

Franklin's posture toward Britain during his eighteen months in America reflected his pride and self-confidence. He was willing to draft proposals to end the war, but they were offered in a spirit of "take it or leave it," with the assumption (shown clearly in his correspondence) that Britain would choose the latter.[4] One cannot date with precision the taciturn Franklin's conversion to the belief in the necessity of independence; he may well have arrived in Philadelphia in May 1775 not yet aware of Lexington and Concord but certain in his own mind that independence was coming. At any rate, there can be no doubt that on the issue of independence he early and consistently stood with the radicals (although characteristically he worked in committee with no one more closely and cordially than Robert Morris, a notorious footdragger on independence). He was also one of the first members of Congress to admit the possibility that America might need foreign help in procuring that independence. One of his first letters as a member of the Committee of Secret Correspondence was to his friend C. G. F. Dumas in Amsterdam. He asked Dumas to discover the disposition of the various courts of Europe toward giving assistance or agreeing to an alliance should it be asked. He described independence as "likely to happen" and said it was possible that after another campaign "we may find it necessary to ask aid of some foreign power."[5]

As the members of Congress gradually abandoned hope for a negotiated settlement with Britain, a consensus formed that America would need foreign assistance, at least for providing the tools of war.[6] Franklin was no more anxious than was John Adams to ask for help, hoping that America could win independence by her own efforts[7]; however, as a member of the Secret Committee, Franklin knew America's almost total dependence on

---

[2] William B. Willcox, ed., *The Papers of Benjamin Franklin* (New Haven and London: Yale University Press, 1959-), 21: 365–68.

[3] Ibid., pp. 408–11. Franklin, however, did make the offer of paying for the tea dumped in Boston harbor if the Coercive Acts were withdrawn, ibid., pp. 586–89.

[4] See in particular "Intended Vindication and Offer of Congress" [before 21 July 1775] and "Resolutions on Trade" [on or before 21 July 1775], Willcox, *Papers of Benjamin Franklin*, 22: 112–20, 126–28.

[5] Franklin to C. G. F. Dumas, 9 December 1775, Willcox, *Papers of Benjamin Franklin*, 22: 288–89.

[6] See James H. Hutson, "Intellectual Foundations of Early American Diplomacy," *Diplomatic History* 1 (1977): 1–19.

[7] See, for example, Franklin to Joseph Priestley, 7 July 1775, Willcox, *Papers of Benjamin Franklin*, 22: 91–93.

foreign munitions, particularly gunpowder.[8] Once the radicals had won the argument over independence, the real debate in Congress was not over whether foreign aid was needed but rather over what should be offered to obtain it. Optimists like John Adams believed that the prospect of American trade would be sufficient inducement to win French aid; pessimists like Richard Henry Lee believed that it would be necessary to offer France help in case Britain regarded French aid to America as a cause of war.[9] In spite of Adams's suspicions of his constancy, Franklin remained in fundamental agreement with the optimists, believing in America's basic strength and favoring as minimal an involvement as possible with foreign powers.[10] After the alliance had been made Franklin was its most ardent defender, but always as a necessary evil to protect America from Britain.

Franklin's selection as one of the commissioners to France meant that any personal reservations about connections with France became irrelevant. His mission was to procure a treaty of amity and commerce. What he could offer was dictated by the instructions of Congress—the promise of neutrality in case France was drawn into war or, if pressed, the promise to give six months' notice before making peace. Only the tactics of how to win French agreement were left to the commissioners.

Franklin's first recorded thoughts on diplomatic tactics were based on threats. The commissioners' instructions encouraged them to use the threat of reconciliation with Britain unless they received an "immediate and explicit declaration of France in our favour."[11] Before Franklin departed for France he drafted a proposal for purchasing Canada, the Bahamas, and Florida from Britain in return for recognition of American independence. He explained his reasons for drawing up the proposal: to divide British public opinion; to provide protection in case he was captured by the British at sea (as later happened to Henry Laurens, American commissioner to the Netherlands); and because "the knowledge of there being powers given to the Commissioners to treat with England, may have some effect in facilitating and expediting the proposed treaty with France."[12] There is no in-

---

[8] Orlando W. Stephenson, "The Supply of Gunpowder in 1776," *American Historical Review* 30 (1925): 271–81. It was primarily to procure arms and ammunition that the Committee of Secret Correspondence commissioned Silas Deane. Committee of Secret Correspondence to Silas Deane: Instructions, 2–3 March 1776, Willcox, *Papers of Benjamin Franklin*, 22: 369–74.

[9] For a succinct description of the two groups see John Adams to John M. Jackson, 30 December 1817, Charles Francis Adams, ed., *The Works of John Adams, Second President of the United States, with a Life of the Author*, 10 vols. (Boston: Little, Brown and Company, 1856), 10: 269. Lee joined the Committee of Secret Correspondence in October, 1776.

[10] See L. H. Butterfield, ed., *Diary and Autobiography of John Adams*, 4 vols. (Cambridge: The Belknap Press of Harvard University Press, 1961), 3: 337–38; Franklin to Arthur Lee, 21 March 1777 (DLC). Note that Franklin argued a year earlier than Paine that by remaining united to Britain America had to fear being dragged into Britain's "plundering Wars." Franklin to Joseph Galloway, 25 February 1775, Willcox, *Papers of Benjamin Franklin*, 21: 509.

[11] Congress to American Commissioners: Instructions, 24 September–22 October 1776, Willcox, *Papers of Benjamin Franklin*, 22: 624–30.

[12] Sketch of propositions for a peace, after 26 September and before 25 October 1776, Willcox, *Papers of Benjamin Franklin*, 22: 630–33.

dication he ever made use of this particular document, but his first approach was only slightly less crude. The French would teach him to use more subtlety.

Without yet appearing in a public capacity (lest either France or America be embarrassed by a French refusal to recognize him), Franklin met Arthur Lee and Silas Deane in Paris just before Christmas of 1776.[13] At their first meeting with French Foreign Minister Vergennes, the commissioners spoke only in generalities and presented Vergennes with a copy of Congress's proposed treaty of commerce.[14] A week later the commissioners were emboldened to have a second audience with Vergennes, at which they gave him a memoir asking for 20,000–30,000 muskets, ammunition, and field pieces to be sent under convoy, plus the loan of eight ships of the line. The commissioners promised that if war should occur, "North America" was ready to guarantee all current French and Spanish possessions in the West Indies as well as those France and Spain might conquer.[15] At first sight this seems to exceed grossly what the commissioners were authorized to give; more likely it was a clumsily phrased offer to guarantee French and Spanish possessions from *American* attack. Franklin accompanied this request with a memoir on the current state of the United States, warning of his apprehensions "that if the Commerce of America is much longer obstructed, the Party who dislike the War will be so strengthen'd as to compel the rest to an Accommodation with Britain."[16] He soon was given a schoolboy's lesson in diplomacy, delivered verbally by Vergennes's undersecretary, Conrad-Alexandre Gérard. Through Gérard, Vergennes explained that open aid would be regarded by Britain as a declaration of war, although this refusal was sweetened by the grant in secrecy of 2,000,000 livres.[17]

The commissioners did not immediately assimilate the lesson. Franklin composed a letter of thanks and an abject apology, but within a month the commissioners renewed their request and their warnings.[18] The money, moreover, appears to have counterbalanced the humiliation. Perhaps encouraged by Spanish Ambassador Aranda, Arthur Lee went uninvited to Spain. There he was treated with contempt, but he came back exultant after being tossed another bone (clothing, gunpowder, and a loan of 187,500

---

[13] William Temple Franklin, *Memoirs of the Life and Writings of Benjamin Franklin*, 3 vols. (London: Henry Colburn, 1818), 1: 309–10; Franklin to Silas Deane, 7 December 1776 (CtHi).

[14] Franklin to Committee of Secret Correspondence, 4 January 1777 (DLC); Vergennes to the conde de Aranda, Spanish ambassador to France, 28 December 1776 (AHN).

[15] American Commissioners to Vergennes, 5 January 1777 (AAE).

[16] See Benjamin Franklin Stevens, ed., *Facsimiles of Manuscripts in European Archives Relating to America, 1775–1783*, 25 vols. (London: privately printed, 1889–1898), 6: no. 614 for Franklin's memoir.

[17] Vergennes to American Commissioners: Procès Verbal, 13 January 1777; rough drafts are Stevens, *Facsimiles of Manuscripts*, 6: nos. 621, 622. See also Vergennes to the marquis d'Ossun, French ambassador to Spain, 12 January 1777 (AAE). "Livre" will stand for *livre tournois*. For its equivalence in contemporary purchasing power see above.

[18] American Commissioners to Gérard, 14 January 1777, Paul P. Hoffman, ed., *Lee Family Papers 1742–1792* (8 rolls of microfilm, Charlottesville: University of Virginia Library, 1966) roll 3, frame 17; American Commissioners to Vergennes, 1 February 1777 (AAE).

livres).[19] A bad example, indeed—Lee soon departed uninvited to Berlin and returned not only empty-handed but with his pockets picked (the British ambassador having stolen his personal papers).[20] His example would be imitated repeatedly as Americans thrust themselves on foreign capitals from The Hague to St. Petersburg. John Adams, one of them, compared himself and his fellow defiers of tradition to militiamen (who successfully defied military tradition)[21]; the more experienced Franklin had reservations. By the time Lee went to Spain, Franklin had conceived doubts about begging for help. He wrote Lee:

While we are asking Aids, it is necessary to gratify the desires, and in some Sort comply with the Humours, of those we apply to. Our Business now is to carry our Point. But I have never yet chang'd the opinion I gave in Congress, that a Virgin State should preserve the Virgin Character, and not go about suitoring for Alliances, but wait with decent Dignity for the Applications of others. I was overrul'd; perhaps for the best.[22]

In spite of Lee's financial success Franklin did not change his mind. To Adams in the Netherlands, to John Jay in Spain, to Francis Dana in Russia his advice was the same: It is not for us to solicit favors; it is for us to grant favors, the favors of our future commerce and markets. Deane and Lee were prone to threaten, but they were also willing on their own to offer France preferences in American trade.[23] Franklin was not willing to offer such inducements for French assistance, and he soon changed his mind about making threats.

Franklin's belief that he could wait for others to approach him seems to have been based on his optimism about the United States, in his eyes a

---

[19] American Commissioners to Committee of Secret Correspondence, 28 April 1777 (MH) and 25 May 1777 (DNA). For rumors Aranda had encouraged the journey see Stevens, *Facsimiles of Manuscripts*, 3: no. 248. Deane planned to go to The Hague but his journey was deferred. American Commissioners to Committee of Secret Correspondence, 6 February 1777 (DNA) and 12 March–9 April 1777 (DNA).

[20] American Commissioners to Baron Schulenburg, 19 April 1777 (DNA) and to the Committee for Foreign Affairs (renamed from Committee of Secret Correspondence, 17 April 1777) 28 April 1777 (MH) and 25 May 1777 (DNA); Arthur Lee to Franklin and Deane, 28 June 1777 (DNA).

[21] John Adams to Robert R. Livingston, 21 February 1782, Francis P. Wharton, ed., *The Revolutionary Diplomatic Correspondence of the United States*, 6 vols. (Washington Government Printing Office, 1889), 5: 196; see also James H. Hutson, *John Adams and the Diplomacy of the American Revolution* (Lexington: The University Press of Kentucky, 1980), pp. 151–54.

[22] Franklin to Arthur Lee, 21 March 1777, Albert Henry Smyth, ed., *The Writings of Benjamin Franklin*, 10 vols. (New York: The Macmillan Company, 1907), 7: 35. Gerald Stourzh, *Benjamin Franklin and American Foreign Policy*, 2d ed. (Chicago: University of Chicago Press, 1969), p. 126, feels Franklin is referring to the commissioners' additional instructions of 16 October 1776 to endeavor to obtain from ministers of foreign states recognition of American independence. These additional instructions also authorized the commissioners to sign treaties of peace, amity, and commerce with states other than France. See Willcox, *Papers of Benjamin Franklin*, 22: 629–30.

[23] Charles Isham, ed., *The Deane Papers (Collections of the New-York Historical Society, 19–23)*, 5 vols. (New York: The New-York Historical Society, 1887–1891), 1:184–95, 361–64; Brian N. Morton and Donald Spinelli, eds., *Beaumarchais Correspondance*, 4 vols. to date (Paris: A.–G. Nizet, 1969–), 2: 171–76.

huge, fertile, well-governed, and potentially rich country. It was only gradually that he developed this belief as a negotiating posture. In January and February the commissioners had depicted for Vergennes a country in danger of collapse unless it received aid; they even took a pledge to exceed their instructions if necessary.[24] In March the commissioners received new instructions from Congress. In exchange for French military assistance they offered a share of the Newfoundland fishery and half of Newfoundland itself, plus American help in conquering the British West Indies.[25] When their proposal was rejected the commissioners elected not to press the offer, explaining:

Feeling ourselves assisted in other Respects cordialy and essentially we are the more readily induced to let them take their own Time, and to avoid making ourselves troublesome by an unseasonable Importunity. The Interest of France and Spain however in securing our Friendship and Commerce seems daily more and more generaly understood here, and we have no doubt of finally obtaining the Establishment of that Commerce with all the Formalities necessary.[26]

The voice clearly is Franklin's but the reason for the new tone of self-confidence is unclear. The negotiations were stalemated, and the commissioners had been given no reason for optimism. My suspicion is that Franklin's adoption of a diplomatic posture based on reserve, no longer issuing either threats or supplications, was the result not of encouragement but of French coolness. The French court was still a court—not as mean-spirited as the British court, but still a bad place for supplicants. Unlike all his wartime colleagues present and future, (Deane, Lee, Adams, and Jay), Franklin's adoption of a diplomatic posture based on reserve, no longer issuing of his two accompanying grandsons away from France to be educated in Geneva as a Presbyterian and a republican.[28] If we cannot be certain what caused his new reserve toward the French government, we do know from the later testimony of Silas Deane that the initial importunities were contrary to Franklin's better judgment:

It is proper to observe that Doctor Franklin was from the first averse to warm and urgent solicitations with the Court of France. His age and experience, as well as his

---

[24] American Commissioners: Resolutions, 2–5 February 1777 (PU). Note that the commissioners' decision of 2 February to offer a pledge to France not to conclude a separate peace was authorized by the commissioners' instructions; moreover there is no evidence they conveyed this offer to Vergennes.

[25] For the causes of Congress's change in mood see below.

[26] American Commissioners to Committee for Foreign Affairs, 25 May 1777 (DNA). For Vergennes's rejection of the Commissioners' offer see Henri Doniol, ed., *Histoire de la participation de la France à l'établissement des États-unis d'Amérique*, 5 vols. and supplement (Paris: Imprimerie Nationale, 1886–1898), 2: 325.

[27] Butterfield, *Adams Diary and Autobiography*, 3: 46–47; 4: 121–22. Franklin later described the French as having foibles but no national vices. Franklin to Josiah Quincy, 22 April 1779 (NjP). For a prewar example of Franklin's relative lack of prejudice see Willcox, *Papers of Benjamin Franklin*, 17: 340.

[28] Franklin to Samuel Cooper, 9 December 1780 (APS-Bache); Franklin to John Quincy Adams, 21 April 1779 (DLC). For an admission by Franklin of his homesickness see Franklin to Catharine Greene, 28 February 1778 (APS).

philosophical temper, led him to prefer a patient perseverance, and to wait events, and to leave the Court of France to act from motives of interest only. He used often to say that America was a new and young state, and, like a virgin, ought to wait for the addresses of other powers, rather than to make even the first advances; and what confirmed him in these sentiments was, his having early in the contest made it a fixed and certain point with him that France would not in any circumstances or situation suffer America to return under the domination of Great Britain.[29]

The policy of reserve thus represented less the evolution of a new policy than the return to the attitudes and approach Franklin had shown in Congress and had unwisely abandoned on his arrival in France. He would not again abandon them in spite of the frustrations of the coming year.[30]

---

[29] Deane: Open Letter to Joseph Reed, 1784, Isham, *Deane Papers*, 5: 438.

[30] An apparent exception to the policy of reserve is a set of memoirs apparently by Franklin urging France to a more forward foreign policy (Stevens, *Facsimiles of Manuscripts* 2: nos. 149–150). The French government, however, may have solicited the memoirs—it quickly published them in its covertly-run periodical the *Affaires de l'Angleterre et de l'Amérique* (cahier XXIV, pp. ccxxi-ccxxxix, published in July 1777) and reproduced much of their argument in a memoir sent soon thereafter to the Spanish court (Doniol, *Participation* 2: 460–469).

Trans. Amer. Phil. Soc.
Vol. 72 Pt. 1, 1982

III. FRANKLIN THE NEGOTIATOR: SECURING THE ALLIANCE

Most of Franklin's first year in France was spent not in the attempt to secure a commercial treaty but in the accomplishment of a number of lesser objectives. These, too, must be considered in appraising Franklin as a negotiator, even if in large part they were a continuation of projects begun by Silas Deane in the summer of 1776.

The first of these inherited responsibilities was that of negotiating a contract to sell American tobacco to the Farmers General, the consortium of businessmen and bankers which among other functions administered the French government's tobacco monopoly. In fact, there was little chance of running large quantities of American tobacco through the British blockade; the commissioners' success in negotiating a contract and securing an advance of 1,000,000 livres was due chiefly to pressure exerted on the Farmers General by the French government.[1]

Franklin also was involved in the successful negotiations to hire as chief engineer for the Continental Army Louis Lebègue de Presle Duportail. Duportail and his staff were major acquisitions, as were Friedrich Wilhelm Augustus von Steuben and Count Pulaski, both of whom Franklin provided with letters of introduction to Washington.[2] In general, however, the importunities of commission seekers were one of the commissioners' worst trials. Deane had created the problem by trying to win friends through granting on his own authority commissions to four Major Generals (du Coudray, de Kalb, du Mauroy, and Lafayette) with full staffs.[3] The resultant disruption of the American army was responsible for Deane's recall by Congress in late 1777; Franklin and his fellow commissioners eventually had to turn away hundreds of applicants for officers' billets they had no authority to fill.[4]

The commissioners also inherited from Deane the proposal of a French naval officer, *capitaine de vaisseau* Jacques Boux, to build in the Netherlands

---

[1] The best account of these negotiations is Jacob M. Price, *France and the Chesapeake: A History of the French Tobacco Monopoly, 1674–1791, and Its Relationship to the British and American Tobacco Trades*, 2 vols. (Ann Arbor: The University of Michigan Press, 1973), 2: 700–717.

[2] American Commissioners: Agreement with Duportail et al., 13 February 1777 (DNA); Benjamin Franklin to George Washington, 29 May and 4 September 1777 (DLC).

[3] For Deane's defense of his action see Charles Isham, ed., *The Deane Papers* (*Collections of the New-York Historical Society*, 19–23), 5 vols. (New York: The New-York Historical Society, 1887–1891), 5: 428–29.

[4] Catherine M. Prelinger, "Less Lucky than Lafayette: A Note on French Applicants to Benjamin Franklin for Commissions in the American Army, 1776–1785," in Joyce Duncan Falk, ed., *Proceedings of the Fourth Annual Meeting of the Western Society for French History* (Santa Barbara, California: Western Society for French History, 1977), pp. 263–71.

frigates with the strength of ships of the line.[5] In military terms the idea was not as foolish as it might seem—Boux's frigates were the forerunners of the U.S.S. *Constitution*.[6] In diplomatic terms, however, the proposal was totally divorced from reality. The Netherlands were subservient to Britain and there was no hope of building, manning, and then sailing American warships from the Netherlands without their being immobilized by British protests.[7] After embroiling Franklin in countless hours of work, one frigate was finally built, ultimately winding up in the navy of South Carolina.[8] She did not sail from Amsterdam until 1781, leaving in her wake expenses, litigation, and ill will. The commissioners did build a smaller frigate at Nantes in 1777 and purchased a second just after the signing of the alliance. These, however, were obtained for the less glamorous purpose of providing escort for supplies which had been purchased by the commissioners.

Deane had been sent to France to obtain uniforms and arms for 25,000 men, 100 field pieces, and goods to help win over the American Indians.[9] In early 1777 Congress raised its demands, asking the commissioners to send without delay 80,000 blankets, 40,000 uniforms and cloth for another 40,000, 100,000 pairs of stockings, 1,000,000 flints, and 200 tons of lead.[10] Deane claimed that the other commissioners left such commercial transactions in his hands,[11] but in fact major decisions even on commercial matters were made jointly.[12] The commissioners assumed responsibility for an enormous variety of purchases,[13] including contracting with several manufacturers for thousands of uniforms. If Deane's subsequent testimony is to be believed, one of the biggest challenges was French businessmen's reluctance to have any dealings with the officious Arthur Lee, who on one occasion objected that the weight of 4 extra buttons and an extra scrap of cloth would fatigue marching soldiers.[14] Nevertheless the supplies, including 40,000 uniforms and 20,000 muskets, eventually were procured and after the signing of the alliance were shipped to America—one of the commissioners' major achievements.[15]

---

[5] See Isham, *Deane Papers*, 1:340–43.

[6] Howard I. Chapelle, *The History of the American Sailing Navy: The Ships and their Development* (New York: W. W. Norton and Company, 1949), pp. 96, 99, 118.

[7] See Richard Henry Lee, ed., *Life of Arthur Lee, LL.D.*, 2 vols. (Boston: Wells and Lilly, 1829), 1: 337–38.

[8] Richard G. Stone, Jr., "'The *South Carolina* We've Lost': The Bizarre Saga of Alexander Gillon and His Frigate," *The American Neptune* 39 (1979): 159–72.

[9] Committee of Secret Correspondence to Silas Deane: Instructions, 2–3 March 1776, William B. Willcox, ed., *The Papers of Benjamin Franklin* (New Haven and London: Yale University Press, 1959-), 22: 369–74.

[10] Congressional resolution of 5 February 1777, Worthington Chauncey Ford et al., eds., *Journals of the Continental Congress, 1774–1789*, 35 vols. (Washington: Library of Congress and National Archives, 1904–1976), 7: 92.

[11] Deane to Beaumarchais, 6 January 1777, Isham, *Deane Papers*, 1: 449–50.

[12] See Isham, *Deane Papers*, 2: 12; 3: 174–75; 5: 418.

[13] For a summary see ibid., 3: 31–33.

[14] Deane's testimony before Congress, 21 December–31 December 1778, ibid., 3: 173–75; Charles M. Andrews, "A Note on the Franklin-Deane Mission to France," *The Yale University Library Gazette* 2(1928): 61.

[15] Of 3,000,000 livres' worth of supplies only 200,000 livres' worth failed to reach America. Jonathan Williams, Jr., to Congress, 10 September 1778 (APS). See also Arthur Lee to Committee

The continuation of Deane's work was a source of frustration and difficulty for the commissioners, but even worse were the consequences of the suggestions he had sent to Congress before Franklin and Lee's arrival. When Franklin left Philadelphia, Congress had not heard from Deane since shortly after his arrival in Bordeaux. Deane's first letters from Paris were lost in transit, but a letter of 1 October arrived to be read in Congress on 21 December 1776.[16] Its arrival could not have been better timed to make an impression on Congress. The British military victories culminating in the drive into New Jersey, so nearly fatal for the Continental Army, were leading Congress to reexamine foreign policy. The "pessimists" like Richard Henry Lee finally gained control. The commissioners' orders were changed; to procure French assistance they were to offer American military cooperation to France—this was the offer the commissioners tendered unsuccessfully the following March.[17] Congress, moreover, eagerly seized a number of Deane's proposals, further altering its foreign policy.

One of the worst of these ideas was that other courts would welcome American representatives. Taking Deane's advice Congress on 30 December 1776 voted to send commissioners to Madrid, Berlin, Vienna, and Florence.[18] The previous year Franklin had received a copy of a translation of Sallust made by the favorite son of the Spanish king, Charles III, and had sent in exchange a copy of the proceedings of Congress.[19] Apparently it was for this reason that Franklin was elected commissioner to Spain; only the good fortune of Arthur Lee's already having gone there spared Franklin an exhausting and futile journey. Eventually Arthur Lee was elected as a replacement commissioner for Spain, his brother William for both the Holy Roman Empire and Prussia, and Ralph Izard, a South Carolina merchant, for Tuscany. None of the three accomplished anything; frustrated and angry at Franklin's reluctance to advance them money, they eventually became his worst enemies.

As another result of Deane's recommendations, Congress authorized the commissioners to initiate hostilities against Portugal for restricting American shipping.[20] Portugal was involved in a colonial border dispute with France's ally, Spain; it was Deane's idea to curry favor with France and Spain by attacking Portuguese shipping. The commissioners did lodge a protest with Portugal for expelling American shipping, but it took several months to be delivered, by which time Spain and Portugal had made

for Foreign Affairs, 9 June 1778, Francis P. Wharton, ed., *The Revolutionary Diplomatic Correspondence of the United States*, 6 vols. (Washington Government Printing Office, 1889), 2: 608–9.

[16] Isham, *Deane Papers*, 1:287–94.

[17] See above. For the new orders see Committee of Secret Correspondence to American Commissioners, 30 December 1776 (APS).

[18] Ford et al., *Journals of the Continental Congress*, 6: 1057–58.

[19] Franklin to Don Gabriel Antonio de Bourbon, 12 December 1775, Willcox, *Papers of Benjamin Franklin*, 22: 298–99.

[20] Ford et al., *Journals of the Continental Congress*, 6:1035–36, 1057.

peace.[21] In addition, Deane led Congress to believe a loan could be obtained from the French government on favorable terms. Congress promptly ordered the commissioners to borrow £2,000,000 sterling at no more than 6 percent interest.[22] This was a gigantic sum, equal to $10,000,000 in specie or 47,000,000 livres. The commissioners had already received a grant of 2,000,000 livres from the French government and an advance of 1,000,000 livres from the Farmers General. Asking for a sum equivalent to more than 10 percent of the French government's annual budget merely made them look ungrateful.[23]

The most dangerous part of Deane's letter of 1 October, however, proved to be his request for blank American naval officers' commissions so that warships could be fitted out in French ports. The Committee of Secret Correspondence responded by promising to send such commissions, "provided the Court of France dislike not the measure." The commissioners, moreover, were authorized to fit out between one and six warships to war upon British property.[24] Franklin's original instructions were to obtain if possible the protection of French ports for American warships; the *Reprisal* (Captain Lambert Wickes), which brought Franklin to France, had taken two prizes en route.[25] Now the commissioners had the responsibility not only of discerning France's wishes, but possibly also of directing American naval operations. The commissioners lacked any knowledge of naval operations,[26] and even ascertaining French intentions required experience they did not have. Direct permission to make war on Britain, of course, was completely out of the question. Franklin admitted at the outset, "It is certainly contrary to their Treaties with Britain to permit the sale of prizes, and we have no regular Means of trying and condemning them."[27] The question of tacit permission was more complex, however, and French ambiguity made the commissioners' job impossible.

This ambiguity was revealed at the commissioners' first meeting with Vergennes. He warned them that disposing of prizes in French ports was contrary to Anglo-French treaties, yet hinted that ways might be found to

---

[21] American Commissioners to the Portuguese ambassador to France, 26 April 1777 and to the viscount de Ponte Lima, 16 July 1777 (DLC); Government of Portugal: Representation, 27 November 1777 (AAE); F. Castrioto to Franklin, 2 December 1777 (APS). See also American Commissioners to Vergennes, 18 March 1777 (AAE); Franklin to Aranda, 7 April 1777 (AHN).

[22] Committee of Secret Correspondence to American Commissioners, 21 December 1776 (APS); Ford et al., *Journals of the Continental Congress*, 6: 1036-37.

[23] American Commissioners to the Committee of Secret Correspondence, 12 March-9 April 1777 (DNA). For the French budget see J. F. Bosher, *French Finances 1770-1795: From Business to Bureaucracy* (Cambridge: Cambridge University Press, 1970), p. 90.

[24] Committee of Secret Correspondence to American Commissioners, 21 December 1776 (APS); Ford et al., *Journals of the Continental Congress*, 6: 1036.

[25] William Bell Clark, *Lambert Wickes, Sea Raider and Diplomat: The Story of a Naval Captain of the Revolution* (New Haven: Yale University Press, 1932), pp. 88-109. A "prize" is a captured merchantman registered in an enemy country. The prize, both ship and cargo, generally was brought into port and sold.

[26] See above. For the impracticality of their suggestions about naval operations see Wickes to American Commissioners, 5 March 1777 (APS).

[27] Franklin to John Hancock, 8 December 1776 (DNA).

evade the prohibition.[28] Vergennes sympathized with the commissioners'
desires, but he had to be extremely careful not to provoke Britain because
the French naval rearmament program was incomplete; a premature war
could destroy the French navy.[29] The commissioners were unaware of this
and disregarded Vergennes's warnings that France was not ready for war.
They instead reported that France, unlike Britain, would have no difficulty
manning her fleet. The French fleet, like Spain's, was nearly ready, they
went on, and the two fleets combined would be superior to that of the
English.[30] Vergennes could hardly risk disabusing the commissioners too
vigorously lest that dangerous information reach Britain. Instead, he managed to create the impression that his objections to American privateering
were not meant seriously.[31]

Only gradually were the commissioners disabused of this idea. Soon after
their meeting with Vergennes, Franklin told Wickes that he and his prizes
would be kindly received, protected, and supplied in all French and Spanish
ports.[32] Indeed, the commissioners were so naive that they permitted an
unemployed American merchant captain to go secretly to England to purchase a packet boat for them. (The British secret service, knowing of the
purchase, did nothing to hinder it, expecting eventually to gain an opportunity to steal the commissioners' dispatches.)[33] Little wonder they were
confused and desirous of guidance from Vergennes; although they permitted Wickes to cruise for prizes, they sought ways to minimize embarrassment to the French government.[34] In early May they received a strong
rebuke from the French government. The port of Dunkirk had been de-

---

[28] Compare the following sources: Vergennes to Ossun, 4 January 1777, Henri Doniol, ed.,
Histoire de la participation de la France à l'établissement des États-Unis d'Amérique, 5 vols. (Paris:
Imprimerie Nationale, 1886–1898), 2: 113–16; Silas Deane to Robert Morris, 23 August 1777,
Isham, *Deane Papers*, 2: 107; Deane's testimony before Congress, 21 December 1778, ibid., 3:
160–61; British Ambassador Stormont to Secretary of State Weymouth, 26 February 1777,
Benjamin Franklin Stevens, ed., *Facsimiles of Manuscripts in European Archives Relating to
America, 1775–1783*, 25 vols. (London: privately printed, 1889–1898), 14: no. 1438.

[29] For details see Jonathan R. Dull, *The French Navy and American Independence: A Study of
Arms and Diplomacy, 1774–1787* (Princeton: Princeton University Press, 1975), pp. 66–89.

[30] American Commissioners to Committee of Secret Correspondence, 12 March–9 April 1777
(DNA); Franklin to Committee of Secret Correspondence, 4 January 1777 (DNA).

[31] Initially Vergennes may not have recognized the seriousness of the danger posed by
American privateers (a rubric also including vessels commanded by officers of the Continental
Navy, whose commissions were not recognized by the British). To his ambassador in London
he remarked that the sale of prizes and harboring of privateers were contrary to articles 15
and 36 of the Treaty of Utrecht. He stated that he expected the American commissioners to
be displeased by the prohibition but that it was left to their dexterity and prudence to suggest
the means of evading it. Vergennes to the marquis de Noailles, 22 March 1777 (AAE). See
Stevens, *Facsimiles of Manuscripts*, 15: no. 1488.

[32] Wickes to the Committee of Secret Correspondence, 24 January 1777, *Papers of the Continental Congress* (204 rolls of microfilm, National Archives and Records Service, 1959) roll 104,
item 78, vol. 23, frames 355–57.

[33] Franklin to Captain Samuel Nicholson, 26 January 1777 (DLC). The commissioners also
authorized the raising of a regiment to occupy a set of islands off Morocco! American Commissioners to Baron de Rullecourt, January 1777 (British Library).

[34] American Commissioners to Vergennes, 1 March 1777 (AAE); Vergennes to American
Commissioners, after 1 March 1777, Stevens, *Facsimiles of Manuscripts*, 15: no. 1452; Franklin
to Dulongprey et Coney, 12 June 1777 (DLC).

militarized by the peace treaties of 1713, 1748, and 1763 and an English commissioner resided there to insure compliance. Gustavus Conyngham, an American who had been given a naval captain's commission by Franklin and his colleagues, was imprudent enough to fit out a cutter in Dunkirk and then return there with prizes. When the British violently protested, the French government briefly placed Conyngham in jail as an object lesson.[35] The lesson was largely ignored, although Franklin did admit in a letter to his son-in-law the imprudence of using Dunkirk.[36]

In spite of their later denials the commissioners continued to act as though cruises could be mounted with impunity from other French ports.[37] They went ahead with plans to send Wickes, now commanding a squadron of three ships, into the Irish Sea. Wickes's cruise was successful enough to draw a storm of protest, first from the British and then from the French to the commissioners. Franklin and Deane sought first to excuse Wickes's conduct and then asked for French convoy protection for his ships so that they could return to America. It is a tribute to Vergennes's forbearance that he proposed the idea to the British.[38]

French feelings about Conyngham could not be so easily disregarded. Released from prison, he was now fitting out another warship in Dunkirk, partly with the commissioners' funds. Deane, acting on behalf of the commissioners, sent his former secretary William Carmichael to Dunkirk with categorical orders to Conyngham. The captain's new ship was to sail to America without cruising for prizes in French waters and was to engage the British only in self-defense or to obtain necessary provisions.[39] The results, however, were disastrously contrary to the commissioners' orders. Conyngham began taking prizes immediately after sailing. Within ten days the British had recaptured one of his prizes manned by a prize crew composed chiefly of Frenchmen.[40] As we shall see, it remains unclear who was responsible for this violation of orders; Conyngham's explanation was that his crew had threatened to mutiny unless he cruised for prizes.[41] Whatever

---

[35] Vergennes to Noailles, 31 May 1777, Stevens, *Facsimiles of Manuscripts*, 15: no. 1543.

[36] Franklin to Richard Bache, 22 May 1777 (CtY); American Commissioners to Committee for Foreign Affairs, 25 May 1777 (DNA).

[37] Compare the commissioners' response to Vergennes, 21 July 1777 (AAE) with their orders to Captain Johnson (of Wickes's squadron), 21 April 1777, Stevens, *Facsimiles of Manuscripts*, 15: no. 1521.

[38] Franklin to Silas Deane, 9 July 1777 (APS); American Commissioners to Vergennes, 17 and 21 July 1777 (AAE); Stormont to Weymouth, 30 July 1777, Stevens, *Facsimiles of Manuscripts*, 16: no. 1591. See also ibid., no. 1594.

[39] William Carmichael to Gustavus Conyngham, 15 July 1777, Robert Wilden Neeser, ed., *Letters and Papers Relating to the Cruises of Gustavus Conyngham, A Captain of the Continental Navy, 1777-1779* (New York: The Naval History Society, 1915), pp. 64–65; Carmichael to American Commissioners, 30 June 1777, Isham, *Deane Papers*, 2: 85–86; Deane to Gérard, 2 June 1777, ibid., 61–63; Deane to Franklin, 22 February 1781 (APS).

[40] Stevens, *Facsimiles of Manuscripts*, 16: no. 1589.

[41] Conyngham to Deane, 17 September 1777, *The Deane Papers: Correspondence between Silas Deane, His Brothers and Their Business and Political Associates 1771-1795* (Collections of the Connecticut Historical Society 22) (Hartford: Connecticut Historical Society, 1930), pp. 112–13 (hereafter cited as *Deane Correspondence*). Deane accepted this excuse; see Deane's narrative read before Congress, 31 December 1778, Isham, *Deane Papers*, 3: 168; Deane to Robert Morris, 23 August 1777, ibid., 2: 109; Deane to Franklin, 22 February 1781 (APS).

the cause, the result was the most severe diplomatic crisis between France and Britain since 1770, a crisis which Vergennes told British Ambassador Stormont had been provoked deliberately by Franklin.[42] Britain threatened immediate war unless all remaining American warships were ordered out of French ports. The French council of state (roughly equivalent to the British Cabinet) recalled the French fishing fleet from Newfoundland, canceled all leaves for naval officers, and offered a face-saving compromise which largely complied with the British wishes.[43] The next month Wickes's ships were ordered out of port into a waiting British squadron, which captured the brig *Lexington;* Wickes's own vessel, the *Reprisal*, foundered in a storm before she could reach America.

However tragic the loss of two ships, at least a European war was averted. War between Britain and France in the summer of 1777 almost certainly would have resulted in disaster for the French navy; quite likely the British navy then could have blockaded America until the Revolution collapsed from lack of munitions. Vergennes was so outraged he refused even to see the commissioners,[44] and only gradually were relations patched up. The handling of naval affairs by Franklin, Deane, and Lee had a second result, almost as serious. The question of who would dispose of captured prizes led to a major split within the American mission. The demarcation of responsibility between the Committee of Secret Correspondence and the Secret Committee had always been unclear. When the former committee appointed Franklin, Deane, and Lee as its representatives in France, the latter committee appointed its own representative to handle American commercial affairs in France. The Secret Committee's representative, the alcoholic half-brother of Robert Morris, soon became embroiled with the commissioners. Eventually there was a triangular battle for authority among the Secret Committee's agent (Thomas Morris), the commissioners' own agent (Franklin's grandnephew Jonathan Williams, Jr.), and a new congressional appointee as joint commercial agent (Arthur Lee's brother William). The squabble divided the commissioners, involved them in a dispute with Robert Morris, and further discredited the American cause.[45] By the autumn of 1777 Deane's and Lee's mutual suspicions had become barely-concealed hatred.[46] The dispute eventually was resolved: Thomas Morris drank himself to death, William Lee went off to Germany, Jonathan Williams, Jr.,

---

[42] Stormont to Weymouth, 16 July 1777, Stevens, *Facsimiles of Manuscripts*, 16: no. 1575. Arthur Lee blamed Deane; see Arthur Lee to Richard Henry Lee, 4 October 1777, ibid., 3: no. 269.

[43] Dull, *French Navy and American Independence*, pp. 75–81; Brian N. Morton, "'Roderigue Hortalez' to the Secret Committee: An Unpublished French Policy Statement of 1777," *The French Review* 50(1977): 875–90.

[44] Arthur Lee to the President of Congress, 10 February 1779, Edward D. Ingraham, ed., *Papers in Relation to the Case of Silas Deane* (Philadelphia: The Seventy-Six Society, 1855), p. 156.

[45] Best account of the dispute is in Robert Rhodes Crout, "The Diplomacy of Trade: The Influence of Commercial Considerations on French Involvement in the Angloamerican War of Independence, 1775–1778" (Ph.D. diss., University of Georgia, 1977), pp. 167–275.

[46] See, for example, Arthur Lee to F. L. Lee, 7 October 1777, R. H. Lee, *Life of Arthur Lee*, 2: 118–19.

stepped down, and the commercial agency was taken over by several merchants appointed (with somewhat dubious legality) by William Lee. The damage, however, had already been done.

Thus far, the history of the American mission has been an account of failure and ineptness. Franklin and his fellow commissioners, however, had enjoyed two successes. First, they had refrained from issuing any categorical demands which would have produced a rupture with France. Second, by cultivating French public opinion they had helped prepare for the later smooth functioning of the alliance. Franklin's importance in winning over the French public merits examination. Unlike his prior efforts to win public support in England, Franklin's campaign was not based on his writings. During his first year in France he contributed two articles to the government-sponsored journal *Affaires de l'Angleterre et de l'Amérique*,[47] perhaps revised a piece for the *London Public Advertiser*,[48] and may have written a piece for a German newsletter.[49] He also assisted his friend the duc de La Rochefoucauld, whose translations of American state constitutions appeared in the *Affaires*, and provided that journal's editor with copies of his past correspondence and literary pieces.[50] Throughout his mission he, like several other Americans, sent information to Dumas to publish in the Netherlands,[51] but his famous press at Passy produced little more than government documents, legal forms, and pieces for amusement.[52] It was John Adams during his mission in the Netherlands in 1780 to 1782 who carried on Franklin's propagandistic tradition. Why didn't Franklin write more? It certainly wasn't declining skill or vigor; his "Supplement to the Boston Independent Chronicle," written in March 1782, was as savage a satire as he ever wrote. Instead, it would seem he was selecting the proper medium for his message. It was at the dinner table rather than the breakfast table that the influential in France formed their opinions; Franklin's living theater was as appropriate to winning over French noblemen as Adams's journalistic propaganda was to winning over Dutch burghers.

It is necessary to be careful lest we overestimate the importance of Adams's and Franklin's efforts. Adams's mission precipitated a political

---

[47] In addition to the memoirs discussed in the last chapter, the piece on American credit in cahier XXIX, pp. cxliii-clv, is his. It was first sent to the Committee on Foreign Affairs to be published; see the commissioners' letter of 8 September 1777 (DNA). All other attributions to him are doubtful.

[48] The "Intended Vindication and Offer" which appeared on 18 July 1777. Willcox, *Papers of Benjamin Franklin*, 22: 112-20.

[49] Durand Echeverria, "'The Sale of the Hessians.' Was Benjamin Franklin the Author?" *Proceedings of the American Philosophical Society* 98(1954): 427-31.

[50] See La Rochefoucauld to Franklin, 20 January 1777 (APS) and Franklin to La Rochefoucauld and the duchesse d'Enville, 25 April 1777 (Bibliothèque Municipale, Mantes, France).

[51] An example is the Pennsylvania Council of Safety's order of 1 January 1777 to treat all prisoners with compassion. The *Gazette de Leide* used this for an article on 27 May 1777 contrasting the American and British treatment of prisoners. See Dumas to Franklin, 23 May 1777. Carmichael and Deane also sent Dumas information for inclusion in the *Gazette de Leide*. Dumas to Carmichael, 3 and 10 July 1777 (APS) and to Deane, 10 July 1777 (APS).

[52] Luther S. Livingston, *Franklin and His Press at Passy* (New York: The Grolier Club, 1914) provides a listing.

crisis in the Netherlands, but it was a battle of Dutch politicians and citizens over Dutch issues.[53] Franklin's endless rounds of dinner parties certainly was more than a "scene of continual discipation [sic]," as Adams later described it.[54] It not only contributed to Franklin's health and longevity (as Adams himself admitted), but also played a vital part in Franklin's campaign with the French nobility. Still, Franklin's role here, as in his diplomacy, was largely passive. He did not have to change opinions. Rather, he had to reinforce existing inclinations and take care not to alienate potential allies. The French nobility (and a small group of bourgeois wealthy enough to share their social status) were the only section of the French public to have influence at court. They did not make government policy but, as Franklin's friend Turgot had learned when he had been finance minister, they could block it quickly. Franklin had to be certain they did not lose their naiveté about the American Revolution. (Franklin seems to have been less aware of the dangerous example set by the American Revolution than was Adams, although perhaps he was simply being silent about it.) Franklin was the perfect revolutionary for the purpose of reassuring the French privileged class: different enough to be interesting but familiar enough not to be frightening, a Philadelphia rustic with years of experience at court, an American who mispronounced their language but could create a splendid *bon mot*. The chief assistance Vergennes found in preparing the country for war was the Anglophobia heightened by the crisis atmosphere of 1777–1778; Franklin helped reinforce this Anglophobia and, more important, helped assure it would not be counterbalanced by fear of dangerous American revolutionaries.[55]

Public adulation was no guarantee of governmental support, however, and by the autumn of 1777 the commissioners had reason for apprehension. Their huge purchases had well surpassed their funds,[56] the French government had expelled American warships, and the question of who was to dispose of prizes had split the mission.[57] News from America also was threatening; on 25 and 26 August the London papers reported the capture of Fort Ticonderoga by General Burgoyne. The commissioners were no

[53] See Simon Schama's masterful *Patriots and Liberators: Revolution in the Netherlands, 1780–1813* (New York: Alfred A. Knopf, 1977).

[54] L. H. Butterfield, ed., *Diary and Autobiography of John Adams*, 4 vols. (Cambridge: The Belknap Press of Harvard University Press, 1961) 4: 118–119; see also L. H. Butterfield and Marc Friedlander, eds., *Adams Family Correspondence*, 4 vols. to date (Cambridge: The Belknap Press of Harvard University Press, 1963–), 3: 130n; John Adams to Sam Adams, 5 December 1778, *Collections of Massachusetts Historical Society* 73(1925): 74.

[55] Franklin also continued to write friends in England about the wickedness of the North ministry and the strength, determination, and unity of America. See for example Franklin to Joseph Priestley, 27 January 1777 (DLC). Franklin indicated he would entertain propositions from the British government but only on terms of independence; the only concession he could envisage would be the maintenance of some commercial advantages for Britain if the two nations entered into some form of federal union. Sir Philip Gibbes: Minutes of Conversation with Franklin, ca. 5 February 1777 (CtY). In a conversation with Gibbes the following January Franklin retracted his statement—see below.

[56] Isham, *Deane Papers*, 3: 177–78; 5:434–37.

[57] Ingraham, *Case of Silas Deane*, p. 173.

longer able to maintain their policy of diplomatic reserve. On 25 September they reminded Vergennes and Aranda of their offer of military cooperation, requested over 7,000,000 livres' worth of supplies, and renewed their appeal for a subsidy or loan of £2,000,000 sterling.[58] The financial situation was so ominous that Franklin advised canceling existing contracts for supplies and selling those on hand, the military situation so ominous that "it was generally believed in France . . . America must accommodate or submit."[59] Deane later confessed that he had been impatient and uneasy at the French government's reserve and ready to "do anything in [his] power to bring that Court into other measures, such as should beyond a question commit them in the dispute."[60] On 30 September Lee read his colleagues part of a letter from his brother Richard Henry warning that "without an alliance with France and Spain, with a considerable loan to support their funds it would be difficult to maintain their independence."[61] The commissioners, moreover, were warned by Vergennes that British Ambassador Stormont had known the contents of one of their memoirs even before it was presented to the French court and that Congress also contained a traitor who was passing information to the British.[62]

Amidst these dangers Franklin continued to put the best face on events. Because the commissioners' dispatches were intercepted by the British, only one letter from Paris was received in Philadelphia between June 1777 and May 1778. It was a personal letter from Franklin to Tom Paine written on 7 October 1777 in which he said, "Our affairs, so far as they are connected with this country, are every day more promising."[63] A week later Franklin wrote his friend in Parliament David Hartley one of his most eloquent and embittered letters rejecting affiliation with Britain as "unfit and unworthy to govern us."[64] Third-party testimony from several sources, unfortunately none very reliable, shows us a Franklin actually preferring America to win independence on her own rather than accept French help![65]

Franklin's optimism in the end proved justified. The commissioners' financial crisis was the first to be relieved. However much Vergennes may have blamed them for the near rupture with Britain, he could not let the Revolution collapse for want of funds. After a vain attempt to win an equal

---

[58] American Commissioners to Vergennes and Aranda, 25 September 1777 (AAE).

[59] Silas Deane: "Open Letter to Joseph Reed," 1784, Isham, *Deane Papers*, 5: 446.

[60] Ibid., 5: 447.

[61] R. H. Lee, *Life of Arthur Lee*, 1: 335.

[62] Ibid., 1: 335–36.

[63] Paine to Deane, 13 February 1779, Isham, *Deane Papers*, 3: 370; see also Committee for Foreign Affairs to American Commissioners, 28 March 1778 (DNA).

[64] Franklin to Hartley, 14 October 1777, Albert Henry Smyth, ed., *The Writings of Benjamin Franklin*, 10 vols. (New York: The Macmillan Company, 1907), 7: 70.

[65] Arthur Lee's Journal, entry for 25 October 1777, R. H. Lee, *Life of Arthur Lee*, 1: 343–44; Paul Wentworth: General Intelligence and Observations, Stevens, *Facsimiles of Manuscripts*, 3: no. 227; the comte de Lauraguais to Vergennes, 20 September 1777, ibid., 18: no. 1691; Bolton (William Carmichael) to "Monsieur Jean Tourville", 1 November 1777, ibid., 3: no. 288; Captain Joseph Hynson to Lt. Col. Edward Smith, 10 December 1777, ibid., 3: no. 314. The last of these sources is particularly suspect, as are Stormont's reports, which do not merit citation.

commitment from Spain, Vergennes at the beginning of November promised that France would loan America 3,000,000 livres during the coming year.[66] The commissioners' credit was restored for the moment, but their long-term prospects were unaltered. On 27 November they debated a course of action. The embittered Deane proposed telling France categorically that unless she agreed to an alliance, America must come to an accommodation with Britain. Arthur Lee reported Franklin's response:

Dr. F was of a different opinion; he could not consent to state that we must give up the contest without their interposition, because the effect of such a declaration upon them was uncertain; it might be taken as a menace, it might make them abandon us in despair or in anger; besides he did not think it true; he was clearly of opinion that we could maintain the contest, and successfully too, without any European assistance; he was satisfied, as he had said formerly, that the less commerce or dependence we had on Europe, the better, for that we should do better without any connexion with it.[67]

Lee agreed with Franklin; a week later the commissioners' disagreement was ended. Jonathan Loring Austin, the 29-year-old secretary of the Massachusetts Board of War, arrived on 4 December with news that seven weeks earlier Burgoyne's entire army had been captured at Saratoga. The commissioners' position suddenly was transformed. On 6 December Vergennes's undersecretary, Gérard, asked them to resubmit their proposal for an alliance.[68] On the same day the North government drafted instructions for the secret service operative Paul Wentworth to ascertain from the commissioners what proposals they thought "the colonies" were likely to accept.[69] Wentworth soon was in Paris meeting with Deane.

The ineptitude of the British government presented Franklin with a chance to play one of his best diplomatic roles: the innocent who may not be as innocent as he pretends. With bland rectitude the commissioners informed Vergennes that Deane had met with Wentworth; Vergennes reacted with apparent panic, telling his own ambassadors that if France did not reach agreement quickly with America, she would settle with Britain

---

[66] Vergennes to Ossun, 3 October 1777, Stevens, *Facsimiles of Manuscripts*, 19: nos. 1711–12; Floridablanca to Ossun, 17 October 1777, ibid., no. 1725; Arthur Lee's Journal, 4 November 1777, R. H. Lee, *Life of Arthur Lee*, 1: 347. Deane fatuously claimed personal credit for arranging the loan, "Open Letter to Joseph Reed," 1784, Isham, *Deane Papers*, 5: 437–42. Vergennes had already told the commissioners they would not be asked to pay for goods provided them by Beaumarchais, American Commissioners to Committee for Foreign Affairs, 7 October 1777 (DNA); see also Stevens, *Facsimiles of Manuscripts*, 19: no. 1757.

[67] Arthur Lee's Journal, 27 November 1777, R. H. Lee, *Life of Arthur Lee*, 1: 354; see also ibid., p. 351; American Commissioners to Committee for Foreign Affairs, 30 November 1777 (DNA). For Deane's anger and hostility toward France see Stevens, *Facsimiles of Manuscripts*, 2: no. 231.

[68] Arthur Lee's Journal, R. H. Lee, *Life of Arthur Lee*, 1: 357–58.

[69] Minutes arranged with Mr. Wentworth, 6 December 1777, Stevens, *Facsimiles of Manuscripts*, 5: no. 484. See also Charles R. Ritcheson, *British Politics and the American Revolution* (Norman: University of Oklahoma Press, 1954), pp. 233–51.

and then the two would attack France.[70] It seems difficult to take Vergennes's fears seriously.[71] French rearmament finally was nearly complete, the time to make a decision on peace or war was pressing, and it seems patently illogical for Vergennes to have expected America to recede from her demand for independence when she had won her greatest victory.[72] One function of the charade probably was to lure Spain into the war, another to overcome King Louis XVI's scruples by convincing him that war was inevitable and that it was necessary to have America on France's side.[73] Whatever were Vergennes's purposes, the American commissioners certainly forwarded the subterfuge by their contacts with Wentworth.

What were the commissioners' purposes in negotiating with the British? The evidence seems to me overwhelming that their objective was still a commercial treaty with France,[74] and to obtain it they were willing to use Wentworth to put pressure on Vergennes. They also were ready to accept the French as allies. Despite Franklin's supposed reluctance to have the French participate in the war, the commissioners offered no resistance to the French demand that a commercial treaty be accompanied by a military alliance. Indeed just the opposite. Gérard announced that France was prepared to sign treaties both of commerce and of military alliance and then proposed terms for the latter. He later reported to Vergennes, "The Deputies applauded this recital with a sort of transport. Mr. Franklin confessed that he saw in it nothing which was not noble and just, and which was not in keeping with the most generous and elevated views."[75] The succeeding negotiations were remarkably free of the quibbling of which the British would complain in 1782.[76] According to Vergennes the major difficulty was

---

[70] Vergennes to the new French ambassador to Spain, the comte de Montmorin, 15 and 20 December 1777, Stevens, *Facsimiles of Manuscripts*, 20: nos. 1780, 1786. Vergennes did complain he was not informed of Franklin's interview on 31 December with James Hutton, a British religious leader, Vergennes to Montmorin, 8 January 1777, ibid., 21: no. 1827. Apparently Vergennes was not informed of Franklin's interviews on 5 January with Sir Philip Gibbes or on 6 January with Wentworth (see below).

[71] Dull, *French Navy and American Independence*, pp. 89–94.

[72] But see also Crout, "Diplomacy of Trade," pp. 12–23, 232–59.

[73] I have been particularly swayed by reading the memoir translated in C. H. Van Tyne, "Influences which Determined the French Government to Make the Treaty with America," *American Historical Review* 21(1916): 532–33. A copy of the original is in the Mémoires et Documents section of AAE, France 446: ff. 351–57 and dates from ca. January 1781. See also Edward S. Corwin, *French Policy and the American Alliance of 1778* (Princeton: Princeton University Press, 1916), pp. 123–48.

[74] Particularly revealing are Sir Philip Gibbes's minutes of the conversation of 5 January (CtY) in which Franklin rejected all ideas of federal union with Britain. See also Wentworth's minutes of his conversation with Franklin, Stevens, *Facsimiles of Manuscripts*, 5: no. 489.

[75] Conrad-Alexandre Gérard: "Relation," 9 January 1781. Stevens, *Facsimiles of Manuscripts*, 21: no. 1831. Gérard continued, "I had dwelt on the conquest of the whole continent, [i.e., Canada] because Mr. Deane had confided to me that this was, according to the Doctor's way of thinking, the most definite reason for forming ties with France, which he is inclined to think, the United States could otherwise do without." (Stevens's translation.) I find it difficult to believe Franklin quite so optimistic about military victory and suspect this was at least partly a bluff.

[76] For the negotiations see Corwin, *French Policy*, pp. 149–54; Meng, *Conrad-Alexander Gérard*, pp. 76–88; Dull, *French Navy*, pp. 95–101. For the British complaints during the peace nego-

the commissioners' desire that the military alliance come into effect immediately rather than when France would choose to consider herself attacked by Britain.[77]

The astute but temperamental Ralph Izard later criticized the commissioners for several points in which he believed their treaties deficient.[78] In their rush to secure the treaties had they been negligent of detail? They did agree to an article prohibiting any American export duties, but Franklin and Deane were strongly opposed on principle to export duties and were not worried about reciprocal concessions.[79] On boundary questions, however, Izard probably was correct. The commissioners fought to obtain a specific recognition of the Americans' right to keep any conquered British territory outside the thirteen states,[80] but by restricting this right to "the northern parts of America, or the islands of Bermuda" France preserved for her ally Spain the opportunity to regain Florida (taken from her by Britain in 1763). The issue of France's conquering Newfoundland or Cape Breton Island was left ambiguous, and an article was inserted in the Treaty of Commerce guaranteeing exclusive French fishing rights off part of Newfoundland. Izard also pointed out that France had drawn back from a promise made by Gérard on 16 December that America would have the right to make a separate peace. Perhaps it is just as well the commissioners did not have Izard's sharp eyes. On all these issues they probably would have lost and merely delayed the treaties. The criticism of historians that the commissioners exceeded their instructions by agreeing to a treaty of alliance is more easily dismissed. No one thought so at the time, and considering the concessions authorized by Congress at the end of 1776, it is difficult to think so now.[81]

Other than a minor textual change the commissioners by late January had accepted the French draft treaty of alliance.[82] The commercial treaty produced a last minute dispute over the articles prohibiting American export duties. Arthur Lee, backed by Izard, threatened to refuse to sign, and

tiations see Edward E. Hale and Edward E. Hale, Jr., eds., *Franklin in France*, 2 vols. (Boston: Roberts Brothers, 1887–1888), 2: 177–78.

[77] Vergennes to Montmorin, 28 January 1777, Stevens, *Facsimiles of Manuscripts*, 21: no. 1853. Since most European alliances were "defensive" it was generally necessary to appear the injured party. In 1778 Austria was "attacked" by Prussia, France by Britain, and Britain by France; in all three cases the injured party's European allies rejected the claim and remained neutral.

[78] Ralph Izard to Henry Laurens, 16 February, 28 June, 25 July, and 12 September 1778, Wharton, *Revolutionary Diplomatic Correspondence*, 2: 497–501, 629–32, 661–63, 710–14; to Arthur Lee, 18 May 1778, ibid., pp. 586–88; to John Adams, 24 September 1778, ibid., pp. 740–42.

[79] Arthur Lee's Journal, 25 January 1777, R. H. Lee, *Life of Arthur Lee*, 1: 383–84; Franklin: "Outline of letters to be written," ca. 29 January 1778 (APS); Franklin to James Lovell, 22 July 1778 (DNA); Deane to President of Congress, 12 October 1778, Wharton, *Revolutionary Diplomatic Correspondence*, 2: 777–78.

[80] Arthur Lee's Journal, 30 December 1777, 21 and 24 January 1778, R. H. Lee, *Life of Arthur Lee*, 1: 372–73, 378–79, 382–83.

[81] See William C. Stinchcombe, *The American Revolution and the French Alliance* (Syracuse: Syracuse University Press, 1969), pp. 11–15.

[82] Arthur Lee's Journal, R. H. Lee, *Life of Arthur Lee*, 1: 388; American Commissioners to Gérard, 27 January 1778 (ViU).

as a compromise Franklin and Deane agreed to leave the final decision to Congress.[83] The treaties were finally signed on 6 February 1778. The commissioners had won their victory. Their greatest accomplishment, it seems to me, was not that of winning over France; the war itself and the completion of French rearmament were what changed French policy. Their chief victory was maintaining their courage to await patiently that change. In a real sense their victory was over themselves.

---

[83] Lee to Franklin and Deane, 30 January 1778 (APS); Franklin and Deane to Gérard, 1 February 1778 (AAE); Arthur Lee's Journal, 2–6 February 1778, R. H. Lee, *Life of Arthur Lee*, 1: 392–94.

TRANS. AMER. PHIL. SOC.
VOL. 72 PT. 1, 1982

IV. FRANKLIN AS HEAD OF MISSION

S hortly after the signing of the treaties John Adams arrived to replace Silas Deane as a commissioner. What he found outraged him: records ill kept, finances jumbled. In one sense it is easy to be amused by Adams's insistence on an orderly revolution; even the American Revolution was not a tea party, although it began with one. There were serious issues, however, involved in Franklin's disorderliness as unofficial head of the American mission in France, the first in status and influence of the three supposed equals.[1] Franklin, Deane, and later Adams lived in the Parisian suburb of Passy with the French businessman Leray de Chaumont. Security was so lax that the American mission was virtually an employment bureau for the British secret service. The commissioners' control over other Americans in France was so loose that Gustavus Conyngham almost started a war. To assess Franklin as a diplomat, we must confront his abysmal record as an administrator.

Today the best-known instance of Franklin's inattention to security is the penetration of the American mission by Edward Bancroft. Bancroft was a friend of Franklin's from London days and as a young man in Connecticut had been a pupil of Silas Deane's. He served the commissioners as an informal secretary and the British secret service as a spy. Particularly damning of Franklin's naiveté are the accusations of historians that Bancroft also recruited as a spy Franklin's fellow commissioner and close friend Silas Deane. The truth, however, is considerably less damaging: Bancroft swindled not only the Americans, but also the British, and Deane was not a spy at all.

In May 1777 James Van Zandt, a British spy using the alias George Lupton, wrote to William Eden, head of the British secret service:

I yesterday discovered under what name Mr. Deane receives his letters from England, tho' twas attended with some risque. He had occasion to go below for something, in the mean while I slipped into his Closet and discovered numbers of letters directed to him under the name of Monsieur Benson.[2]

Van Zandt's intelligence is of critical importance to historians since it was "Benson" who forewarned King George III of the signing of the Franco-American alliance. On 3 February 1778, three days before the conclusion of the treaties, George wrote Lord North, "Undoubtedly if the intelligence

---

[1] In his autobiography Franklin confessed that orderliness was not one of his virtues: Leonard W. Labaree, ed., *The Autobiography of Benjamin Franklin* (New Haven and London: Yale University Press, 1964), pp. 155–56.

[2] Benjamin Franklin Stevens, ed., *Facsimiles of Manuscripts in European Archives Relating to America, 1775–1783*, 25 vols. (London: privately printed, 1889–1898), 2: no. 162.

sent by Benson is founded, France has taken her part and a War with G. Britain must soon follow."[3] Van Zandt, however, was wrong. Deane was not Benson. The letters he saw had been sent not to Deane but to Deane's partner in playing the London stock market, Edward Bancroft. Solving the mystery of Benson not only clears Deane of the charge of spying but also uncovers many details of the operations of the British secret service.

Among Franklin's papers in the Bache collection of the American Philosophical Society are four letters written in December 1776 and January 1777 by Franklin's former business associate, Samuel Wharton. It is obvious from reading them that two are to Franklin and the other two are to Bancroft under the name of Monsieur Benson. Wharton even suggested that Franklin also adopt an alias in case the British intercepted Wharton's letters. (Franklin obliged by taking the name Monsieur François.)[4] The four letters (and the letters to M. François) are perfectly innocent—Franklin thought so little of them that he filed them with the rest of his correspondence. In fact, he considered the correspondence between Wharton and "Benson" so innocent that when Bancroft was out of town he was willing to pick up mail addressed to Bancroft as "Benson." On 27 December 1778 he wrote Edmé-Jacques Genet, head of Vergennes's bureau of interpreters and editor of the *Affaires de l'Angleterre et de l'Amérique*, "If any News Papers should come to your Hands from London directed to Mr. Benson, they are for me and I shall be oblig'd to you for sending them to me."[5]

The correspondence between Wharton and Bancroft, however, was not as innocent as Franklin believed. Far different were six letters from Wharton to Bancroft intercepted by William Eden's British post office operatives.[6] Their subject is stockjobbing, the use of inside information provided Wharton by Bancroft so the two could speculate on the stock market.[7] Eden had good reason to intercept the correspondence. Bancroft (whose secret service alias was Mr. Edwards) was using his best information to play the stock market, and much to King George's disgust was providing the secret service with the leftovers.[8] We have eyewitness evidence that Bancroft provided Wharton with advance news of the signing of the treaties. An American ship captain named Livingston certified that while in London he was shown a letter dated 27 January 1778, which he was informed had been written

---

[3] Sir John Fortescue, ed., *The Correspondence of King George the Third from 1760 to December 1783*, 6 vols. (London: Macmillan and Company, 1927–1928), 4: 34.

[4] Wharton to M. François, 23 March 1778 (APS). He also used the alias of Mr. Moses in corresponding with Thomas Walpole, another associate in the Walpole Company (see below): Franklin's comments on Thomas Walpole to Edward Bancroft, 7 July 1778 (NN).

[5] Franklin to Genet, 24 December 1778 (DLC).

[6] They are to be found in the British Library, Add. MSS. 24, 321, ff. 6–35.

[7] Two of the letters were addressed to M. St. Pierre, another alias used by Bancroft. See Stevens, *Facsimiles of Manuscripts*, 19: no. 1756. One of Eden's operatives supposedly copied a passage from a letter to "Benson" carried by Bancroft's mistress: see ibid., 2: nos. 137, 138; 8: no. 768; Lewis Einstein, *Divided Loyalties: Americans in England during the War of Independence* (London: Cobden - Sanderson, 1933), p. 414; L. H. Butterfield, ed., *Diary and Autobiography of John Adams*, 4 vols. (Cambridge: The Belknap Press of Harvard University Press, 1961), 4: 74.

[8] See King George III to Lord North, 27 September and 31 December 1777, Fortescue, *Correspondence of King George the Third*, 3: 481–82, 532.

by Dr. Bancroft to Mr. Wharton. According to Livingston the letter informed Wharton

he might depend on it, he had it from the very best authority that the treaty with the Court of France was to be signed the 5th or 6th of February, and desiring him to make his speculations accordingly; in the above words, or words to that effect.

Captain Livingston further certified that he was familiar with Bancroft's handwriting, and he believed the handwriting to be his.[9] Livingston's testimony is corroborated by entries in Bancroft's abstract of his account with Deane. Bancroft recorded that he had paid £420 to "S. Wh."; in case there was a treaty of alliance between France and the United States, "E.B." and "S.D." would receive £1000.[10] King George's remark quoted earlier thus has a note of sarcasm; it was not as Mr. Edwards, the secret service operative, that Bancroft sent news of the treaties—it was instead as Benson the stock-jobber. For George to receive the intelligence it had to be intercepted by the post office[11]; Benson the spy never existed.[12]

We now can understand why Deane was keeping Bancroft's mail. The two men were involved in a partnership to use their inside information to wager on the London stock market. Wharton was one of their London contacts; another probably was Thomas Walpole, a partner of Bancroft, Wharton, and Franklin in the Walpole Company, a concern formed to win land grants in the American West.[13] The scheme to wager on the alliance appears to have originated with Wharton[14]; Bancroft, to whom the suggestion was made, apparently brought in Deane. Deane, moreover, seems to have speculated further on his own. He admitted that he had paid 19,500 livres to Wharton on 17 February 1778,[15] a payment which he never sat-

---

[9] This certificate was printed in the *Pennsylvania Packet*, 17 August 1779. Charles Isham, ed., *The Deane Papers* (Collections of the New-York Historical Society, 19–23), 5 vols. (New York: The New-York Historical Society, 1887–1891), 4: 63–64. For the original see Paul P. Hoffman, ed., *Lee Family Papers 1742–1792* (8 rolls of microfilm, Charlottesville: University of Virginia Library, 1966) roll 4, frames 434–35.

[10] Bancroft and Deane: Abstract of Account, ca. May 1779 (CtHi).

[11] For intelligence that was provided Eden by Bancroft see Stevens, *Facsimiles of Manuscripts*, 5: no. 492; 22: no. 1881. See also Samuel Flagg Bemis, "British Secret Service and the French-American Alliance," *American Historical Review* 29(1924): 492–95.

[12] There are two false leads in the Benson case. First is the fact that Deane traveled from Bordeaux to Paris in July 1776 with someone named Benson (Isham, *Deane Papers*, 1: 169). Second is Stormont's suggestion to his superiors that the House of Benson in Bordeaux might provide intelligence. (Stevens, *Facsimiles of Manuscripts*, 13: no. 1368). Professor L. M. Cullen of Trinity College, Dublin, was kind enough to trace these Bensons who respectively were named Peter, Paul, and James, were from a transplanted Cork family and were, as far as I can determine, totally innocent of involvement with the British secret service.

[13] Bancroft to Walpole, undated, Stevens, *Facsimiles of Manuscripts*, 3: no. 289; Wentworth to Eden, 11 December 1777, ibid., 2: no. 225. Walpole visited Deane in Paris in July 1776. Jacob M. Price, *France and the Chesapeake: A History of the French Tobacco Monopoly, 1674–1791, and Its Relationship to the British and American Tobacco Trades*, 2 vols. (Ann Arbor: The University of Michigan Press, 1973), 2: 704.

[14] —— (Samuel Wharton?) to Bancroft, 10 November 1777, Stevens, *Facsimiles of Manuscripts*, 3: no. 301. The British post office, which intercepted this letter, reported it was from a J. W., probably a misreading of S. W.

[15] Isham, *Deane Papers*, 3: 28.

isfactorily explained. Finally, E. James Ferguson has uncovered evidence that Deane made 20,000 livres speculating on the British market through a Dutch banking house.[16]

If Deane was using his inside information for speculation, why then can we not assume he was also sharing Bancroft's takings from the British secret service? Did he not know his friend and partner was regularly providing intelligence to the British ambassador in Paris? Perhaps so, but there is no documentary evidence for Deane's knowledge of Bancroft's spying, and the evidence of Deane's character is against it. It is a shame Sinclair Lewis was not asked to write the entry for Deane in the *Dictionary of American Biography*. Deane seems a forerunner of Lewis's small-town American businessman. He was self-important, not particularly bright and not quite honest, a convivial and patriotic small-town boy from Wethersfield, Connecticut, suddenly transported to Versailles.[17] This Connecticut Yankee was totally unfitted for King Louis's court; during the few months he was on his own he gave money to a pyromaniac to burn down the British dockyards, encouraged Congress to attack Portuguese shipping, and became involved in a scheme to replace George Washington as commander of the Continental Army with a French nobleman.[18] To place any faith in Deane's intellect seems extremely risky; Bancroft was able to fool Franklin and later Jefferson. Since spying was only a sideline to Bancroft's speculations, it is understandable he could also have deceived Deane.[19]

There is an element of irony in Deane's story. When he returned to America he was accused of diverting public funds to ship goods on his own account, of which action apparently he was innocent. There is no more outraged innocence than that of the criminal accused of a crime he has not committed; Deane was so embittered by his treatment by Congress that in 1781 he wrote a series of defeatist letters in exchange for £3,000 of goods from the British.[20] A shocked Franklin then broke off relations with him; Deane protested his innocence and, given his limitless capacity for self-deception, may well have believed it.[21]

---

[16] E. James Ferguson, *The Power of the Purse: A History of American Public Finance, 1776–1790* (Chapel Hill: University of North Carolina Press, 1961), pp. 89–90. Deane was also rumored to be involved with his friend Beaumarchais in speculation. Stevens, *Facsimiles of Manuscripts* 21: no. 1818. For William Lee's involvement in a similar scheme see Worthington Chauncey Ford, ed., *Letters of William Lee*, 3 vols. (Brooklyn: Historical Printing Club, 1891), 1: 284–86, 341–43.

[17] See the characterization of him in Stevens, *Facsimiles of Manuscripts*, 3: no. 248. The best study of his prior career is Kalman Goldstein, "Silas Deane: Preparation for Rascality," *The Historian* 43 (1980–1981): 75–97.

[18] See William Bell Clark, "John the Painter," *Pennsylvania Magazine of History and Biography* 63(1939): 1–23; Isham, *Deane Papers*, 1: 247; Louis Gottschalk, *Lafayette Comes to America* (Chicago: University of Chicago Press, 1935), pp. 66–82.

[19] See Einstein, *Divided Loyalties*, pp. 47–48. John Adams, who suspected everybody, guessed correctly in the case of Bancroft. See Butterfield, *Adams Diary and Autobiography*, 3: 340.

[20] A succinct account of Deane's treason is in Carl Van Doren, *Secret History of the American Revolution* (New York: The Viking Press, 1941), pp. 417–18. The letters are in volume 4 of Isham, *Deane Papers*.

[21] Franklin had described Deane as "an able, faithful, active, and extremely useful servant of the Publick." Franklin to James Lovell, 21 December 1777 (DNA). After Deane's letters

Assuming that Deane was too unintelligent to be useful to the British and Bancroft too self-interested, it would seem that Franklin's bad judgment and naiveté did no harm. Unfortunately on another subject involving Deane Franklin cannot be let off so easily. There is evidence to suggest that Deane was responsible for Conyngham's nearly disastrous cruise, and there is even stronger evidence implicating Deane's personal secretary, William Carmichael.

Carmichael remains a remarkably mysterious figure, given his later prominence as a congressman and as the American representative at the court of Spain. We do not even know the year of his birth. We do know that in June 1776 the young and wealthy Carmichael, after completing his studies at the University of Edinburgh, was in London pursuing shared interests with several American ship captains.[22] In London Carmichael met Arthur Lee, a graduate of Edinburgh, colonial agent, and now intelligence source for the Committee of Secret Correspondence. Lee entrusted Carmichael with a letter to the committee (consisting of misinformation and character assassination)[23] and Carmichael departed for Nantes. En route he fell ill in Paris where he soon met the newly arrived Silas Deane, Lee's rival as intermediary with the French government. Carmichael quickly shifted allegiances, showing Lee's letter to Deane and becoming Deane's private secretary.[24] That autumn Deane sent Carmichael to Amsterdam and Berlin, supposedly to gather intelligence and find sources of credit for his public activities, but quite likely also to further Deane's grandiose plans to construct an international cartel to handle trade with America.[25] In January 1777 the commissioners sent him to Le Havre to inspect the arms and clothing being sent to America by Deane and Caron de Beaumarchais.[26] (The playwright Beaumarchais was head of Roderigue Hortalez and Company, the shipping concern capitalized by the French government for making clandestine arms shipments.) Increasingly Carmichael became the commissioners' representative on mission, his position obviously not harmed

---

Franklin chastized his conduct but urged that he be treated fairly by Congress. Franklin to Livingston, 4 March 1782 (DNA); Franklin to Morris, 30 March 1782 (DLC) and 14 December 1782 (Ct); Franklin to Deane, 19 April 1782 (Mrs. Archibald S. Crossley); Franklin: certificate, 18 December 1782, Isham, *Deane Papers*, 5: 116–117.

[22] See Stevens, *Facsimiles of Manuscripts*, 1: nos. 16, 20, 44, 49; 2: nos. 143, 242; 3: nos. 243, 245; 7: no. 657 for the correspondence of Carmichael and Captains Hynson and Nicholson with their English mistresses. This correspondence was being monitored by the British secret service, whose chief operative for this sort of work was the Reverend John Vardill. For his service to the crown Vardill was named a professor of divinity. Einstein, *Divided Loyalties*, pp. 51–67, 409–17.

[23] Francis P. Wharton, ed., *The Revolutionary Diplomatic Correspondence of the United States*, 6 vols. (Washington Government Printing Office, 1889), 2: 95–96.

[24] The letter did not reach America until 1778, by which time Lee had become Carmichael's bitter enemy. See Carmichael to Franklin, 1 February 1778 (APS); Isham, *Deane Papers*, 2: 491–92; 3: 154–56, 182–83; 5: 378; Edward D. Ingraham, ed., *Papers in Relation to the Case of Silas Deane* (Philadelphia: The Seventy-Six Society, 1855), pp. 137–40. Lee later described Carmichael as "subtle, insinuating, false, persevering, and ambitious." Isham, *Deane Papers*, 4: 99.

[25] Isham, *Deane Papers*, 1: 176, 233–35, 286, 311–13, 326, 351–54, 393, 400, 421–22; 3: 158; 5: 393, 403.

[26] Ibid., 1: 451–52, 461–63, 471–74.

by his friendship with Franklin's grandson and secretary, William Temple Franklin. While not on special missions Carmichael was at the center of a social life differing greatly from the salons and dinner parties attended by the elder Franklin. Carmichael's circle was based on the less elevated pleasures of unemployed ship captains and of young Americans supposedly in Europe for their education. It was also the gathering place of several operatives of Eden's secret service.

Three of these operatives were close friends of Carmichael's: Edward Bancroft,[27] James Van Zandt (who went through Deane's papers),[28] and Joseph Hynson, an unemployed ship captain. Around the beginning of March 1777 Hynson passed word to his secret service contact, Lieutenant Colonel Edward Smith, that Carmichael was anxious to cooperate with Smith. Furthermore, Hynson stated Carmichael had hinted to him that if it were "absolutely useful" to Hynson, he would let him steal documents from the American mission.[29] The lead was so promising that before Smith returned to England he convinced Lord Stormont, the British ambassador in Paris, to contact Carmichael. Carmichael held two meetings with Thomas Jeans, the ambassador's chaplain, and at least one with the ambassador's secretary.[30] Hynson was also in contact with Stormont; he and Carmichael reported their meetings to the American commissioners with a cover story that the British government wished to see if the rebellion could be ended by the offer of terms short of independence. (Carmichael naturally said he had rebuffed the offer on behalf of the commissioners.) Carmichael's cover story was so plausible that Franklin and Deane passed it on to Vergennes, who encouraged the meetings to continue.[31] The results of the meetings are a mystery. Although there is no evidence that Carmichael agreed to become a British agent, it appears he later did furnish information to Wentworth.[32] Whether Carmichael provided information is not, however, the critical issue. The American mission was so full of people stealing information it is surprising they did not trip over each other. (Hynson eventually made the major steal: several months' worth of dispatches about to leave for America, which he replaced with blank sheets of paper.) The greatest danger

---

[27] Stevens, *Facsimiles of Manuscripts*, 1: no. 10; 5: no. 474.

[28] Ibid., 1: no. 10. Van Zandt was the son of a prominent New York merchant and patriot and the brother of a captured Continental Army officer. See *New-York Historical Society Collections* 14(1905): 155 and Harold C. Syrett, ed., *The Papers of Alexander Hamilton*, 26 vols. (New York and London: Columbia University Press, 1961–1979), 1: 471.

[29] Stevens, *Facsimiles of Manuscripts*, 3: no. 248; 7: no. 670.

[30] Jeans to Smith, 27 March 1777, ibid., no. 246; Vergennes to Gérard, 31 March 1777, ibid., 7: no. 672; Gérard to Vergennes, 3 April 1777, ibid., 7: no. 675. A note setting up Jeans and Carmichael's first meeting, probably in the hand of Stormont's secretary, is in the University of Pennsylvania Library. The story is complicated by Stevens, who confuses Jeans with the secretary; for proper identification of Jeans see Stevens, *Facsimiles of Manuscripts*, 3: no. 332 and 3: no. 315.

[31] See in particular Gérard's report of 3 April 1777, ibid., 7: no. 675.

[32] Ibid., 3: no. 317; see also ibid., no. 314. Note, however, that a letter to Wentworth of 24 April 1777 (British Library: Add MSS 24,322: f.20) attributed to Carmichael is actually from Bancroft (Stevens, *Facsimiles of Manuscripts*, 1: no. 65). Bancroft moreover reported that Ambassador Stormont's attempts to suborn Carmichael had failed. Ibid., 3: no. 250.

came from Carmichael's motivation in making contact with the British. The young Marylander was rich enough to serve the American mission without pay; indeed, he told his friend Van Zandt he had advanced the commissioners nearly £1,000.[33] If he did volunteer his services to Stormont, his chief motive almost certainly was not greed, but rather his openly expressed hatred of France.

Carmichael was anything but reluctant in expressing his political views. His correspondence is a long diatribe against France for not being more forward in helping the United States. Gradually Carmichael revealed his goal—to bring about a reconciliation between the United States and Britain through provoking an Anglo-French war (which would force Britain to make concessions in order to purchase American help).[34] Finally Carmichael revealed the means by which this could be accomplished: by sending American privateers from French ports to provoke Britain into war against France.[35] Carmichael's proposal may not have been mere fancy. It was Carmichael whom Franklin and his fellow commissioners selected to deliver Conyngham's final orders!

There is strong evidence that Carmichael ordered Conyngham to disregard the commissioners' explicit orders not to take prizes. In a postscript written from Dunkirk, Carmichael told William Bingham, the congressional agent in Martinique, that he was dispatching Conyngham to destroy English shipping.[36] Conyngham himself later testified he had been given verbal orders which could not be committed to paper.[37] The real question would seem to be not Carmichael's complicity but whether he was acting on his own.

This question is unanswerable. We know that it was Deane who drafted Conyngham's instructions.[38] Deane was capable of any rashness; later he confessed that in 1777 he had been willing to do anything to bring France into the war and that he had exercised bad judgment.[39] Did Carmichael deliver his own verbal orders to Conyngham because of his hatred of

---

[33] Van Zandt (Lupton) to Eden, 23 September 1777, ibid., 2: no. 199. Deane later denied Carmichael had ever advanced money. Deane to Carmichael, 30 June 1784, Isham, *Deane Papers*, 5: 318-22. See also ibid., 3: 196.

[34] Carmichael to C. G. F. Dumas, 21 January 1777, Isham, *Deane Papers*, 1: 465-67; 21 April 1777, ibid., 2: 48-49; 28 April 1777, Wharton, *Revolutionary Diplomatic Correspondence*, 2: 308-9; 9 May 1777, ibid., 2: 318-19; 13 June 1777, ibid., 2: 338; 20 June 1777, Isham, *Deane Papers*, 2: 73-76; Carmichael to William Bingham, 25 June-6 July 1777, Wharton, *Revolutionary Diplomatic Correspondence*, 2: 346-49. For the vehemence of Carmichael's animosity against the French see also Stevens, *Facsimiles of Manuscripts*, 2: no. 168.

[35] Carmichael to Bingham, 25 June-6 July 1777, Wharton, *Revolutionary Diplomatic Correspondence*, 2: 346-49.

[36] Ibid. Carmichael also proposed to Bingham that the latter should send American privateers from Martinique to provoke hostilities.

[37] "Narrative of Captain Gustavus Conyngham, U.S.N., while in Command of the 'Surprise' and 'Revenge,' 1777-1779," *Pennsylvania Magazine of History and Biography* 22(1898): 480.

[38] Deane to Franklin, 22 July 1777 (APS); Arthur Lee to Robert Morris, 4 October 1777; Stevens, *Facsimiles of Manuscripts*, 19: no. 1714.

[39] Deane: Open Letter to Joseph Reed, 1784, Isham, *Deane Papers*, 5: 447. See above for quotation from this source. It should be noted that Deane was writing of his mood in the autumn of 1777, which weakens the case against him.

France, or was he merely the agent of Deane?[40] It is doubtful we ever will know.

Carmichael's career was just beginning, although his stay in France soon ended. Vergennes suspected him of passing information to the British minister in the Netherlands.[41] Carmichael being no longer welcome in France, the commissioners decided to testify their confidence in him by sending him back to America with dispatches. The news of Saratoga intervened, however, and they instead decided to send Silas Deane's brother Simeon with the news that France intended to recognize American independence. Carmichael was outraged at what he regarded as an insult by his friend Silas Deane. When Carmichael arrived in Philadelphia, his closed-door testimony reinforced Congress's suspicions about Deane's probity and prevented the settling of his accounts.[42] (Carmichael also testified that the French regarded Arthur Lee as suspicious.)[43] Carmichael later served as congressman from Maryland, secretary to John Jay on his mission to Spain, and American chargé d'affaires at the Spanish court[44]; like the courteous and obliging Edward Bancroft, he remained Franklin's lifelong friend.[45]

Bancroft, Carmichael, Hynson, and Van Zandt are not the only examples of the commissioners' misguided trust. Others include Thomas Digges, who embezzled money Franklin had sent him for prisoner relief,[46] and Lee's secretaries, John Thornton and Hezekiah Ford, respectively a stockjobber/ British agent and a suspected loyalist.[47] The best judgment shown by the

---

[40] Lee claimed Deane was fully responsible. See Stevens, *Facsimiles of Manuscripts*, 3: no. 269; 19: no. 1714. We know that Deane wrote Conyngham on 9 July but the letter has disappeared. See *Papers of the Continental Congress* (204 rolls of microfilm, National Archives and Records Service, 1959) roll 115, item 87, vol. 21, frame 201. The commissioners showed no suspicion that Carmichael had violated orders. Another theory can be more easily dismissed. Clark, *Lambert Wickes*, pp. 187–93 suggests Lambert Wickes was the instigator of a plan to provoke war by cruising against the English. In fact Wickes's letters betray an almost pathetic desire that he be sent clear orders by the commissioners and a preference for returning to America. See, for example, Wickes to American Commissioners, 28 February and 4 July 1777 (APS) and to the Committee of Secret Correspondence, 28 February 1777, William Bell Clark and William James Morgan, eds., *Naval Documents of the American Revolution*, 8 vols. to date (Washington: Department of the Navy, 1964–) 8: 622.

[41] This was actually Bancroft's work. See Paul Wentworth to the earl of Suffolk, 16 November 1777, Stevens, *Facsimiles of Manuscripts*, 2: no. 218.

[42] Richard Henry Lee, ed., *Life of Arthur Lee, LL.D.*, 2 vols. (Boston: Wells and Lilly, 1829), 1: 367; Stevens, *Facsimiles of Manuscripts*, 20: no. 1759; Isham, *Deane Papers*, 2: 498–99; 3: 446–48; Worthington Chauncey Ford et al., eds., *Journals of the Continental Congress, 1774–1789*, 35 vols. (Washington: Library of Congress and National Archives, 1904–1976), 12: 927–28.

[43] Carmichael to Franklin, 22 April 1780 (DLC).

[44] Samuel Gwynn Coe, "The Mission of William Carmichael to Spain" (Ph.D. diss., Johns Hopkins University, 1926); Floyd B. Streeter, "The Diplomatic Career of William Carmichael," *Maryland Historical Magazine* 8(1913): 119–40.

[45] See particularly Franklin to Carmichael, 8 February 1778 (DNA). For other testimony about Carmichael see Ford, *Letters of William Lee*, 2: 355; Butterfield, *Adams Diary and Autobiography*, 4: 77.

[46] William Bell Clark, "In Defense of Thomas Digges," *Pennsylvania Magazine of History and Biography* 77(1953): 381–438.

[47] Fortescue, *Correspondence of George the Third*, 3: 180–81; 4: 46–47; Isham, *Deane Papers*, 3: 63–65, 180–81; Wharton, *Revolutionary Diplomatic Correspondence*, 1: 539–40; Ford et al., *Journals of the Continental Congress*, 13: 116. Franklin wrote a letter of recommendation for Ford to Pierre Landais, 25 April 1779 (ViU).

commissioners was the choice of Franklin's grandson as their secretary and Franklin's grandnephew as their agent in Nantes; once they had mastered their jobs, William Temple Franklin and Jonathan Williams, Jr., proved competent, diligent, reliable, honest, and patriotic.[48]

How did Franklin and his colleagues make so many egregious misjudgments of character? One answer can be dismissed: the accusation that Franklin was not fully loyal to the American cause represents little more than rumor-mongering. Such suspicions rest on the fact that Franklin remained a member of a British land speculating company, ignoring the facts that Franklin's investment was less than £300, that he withdrew the funds he had left in England for lobbying Parliament on its behalf and instead lobbied Congress, and that he donated his salary as postmaster general to disabled American war veterans and invested £3000 in American loan office certificates.[49] More important, allegations of this type overlook Franklin's anger at Britain, expressed in many dozen letters, Franklin's confidence in American victory, unwavering in the worst of crises, and Franklin's advocacy of *American* rights to western lands, unyielding during the peace negotiations. To accuse Franklin of disloyalty requires a sweeping disregard of evidence.

How then do we account for Franklin's blindness? A clue may be found in a letter he wrote in response to a warning that he was surrounded by spies. He replied that he had no doubts the information was well founded, but that he could do nothing about it. His rule was to have no secrets he would not want revealed: "If I was sure therefore my Valet de Place was a spy, as probably he is, I think I should not discharge him for that, if in other Respects I lik'd him." After the word "spy" he had written and then deleted "and I like."[50] Franklin's response is revealing. One of his most pronounced characteristics was his unswerving loyalty to his friends. Until presented with irrefutable evidence he could believe no evil of a friend, making all the more bitter the defection of a Deane or Digges to whom he had given his trust. This faith in others is appealing in human terms, but it was a major failing for someone entrusted with so much responsibility.

Franklin may have been vulnerable to deception for other reasons as well. He liked to be surrounded by polished, ambitious, and clever young

---

[48] For Williams's services see his letter to Congress of 10 September 1778 (APS). Franklin took great care that he not be accused of favoring his relatives at the expense of the public; see, for example, Franklin to Williams, 23 March 1782 (DLC). Williams amply justified Franklin's trust as did Temple Franklin; for a testimony to the latter see Adams to Arthur Lee, 10 October 1778, Wharton, *Revolutionary Diplomatic Correspondence*, 2: 760–61.

[49] Franklin's Endorsement of Legal Opinions on Land Titles Obtained from the Indians, 12 July 1775, William B. Willcox, ed., *Papers of Benjamin Franklin* (New Haven and London: Yale University Press, 1959–), 22: 102–3; Franklin: Note on the extract of a letter from Thomas Walpole to Edward Bancroft, 14 July 1778 (NN); Franklin to Thomas Walpole, 12 January 1777 (David Holland, House of Commons Library); Walpole to Franklin, 10 February 1777 (APS); Franklin to William Strahan, 3 October 1775, Willcox, *Papers of Benjamin Franklin*, 22: 218–19; Richard Bache to Franklin, 5 February 1777 (APS-Bache); Franklin to Jan Ingenhousz, 11 February 1788 (APS).

[50] Franklin to Juliana Ritchie (draft), 19 January 1777 (APS). This was written in response to her letter to him of 12 January 1777 (APS).

men like William Carmichael, perhaps reminders of his youth.[51] Further-more, Franklin had to hold himself and his relatives to standards of financial probity rather exceptional in eighteenth-century terms. He needed to watch himself continually to prevent any signs of weakness or doubt and, in spite of his gallantry, to avoid scandal. The reverse of the strict demands he made on himself was a tolerance for the foibles of others (except those like his younger grandson Benny and Benny's schoolboy friends, for whom Frank-lin felt responsible).[52] To have tightened up security procedures would have required a major psychological adjustment. When necessary he was willing to make such adjustments; during the peace negotiations the gregarious Franklin gave up his custom of entertaining his fellow Americans every Sunday.[53] His need for the comfort of friends then revealed itself in a series of highly emotional letters written to friends in England about the evils of war. I doubt Franklin could have borne such a strain indefinitely; his functioning as a diplomat was dependent on the loose and convivial at-mosphere which undermined security and made the French so reluctant to trust the Americans.[54]

Perhaps in the end Franklin's failings were those of the Revolution itself. Congress after all could have tightened security by providing the American mission with an adequate, loyal, well-paid professional staff. Congress did not; it functioned by using the materials at hand (including human ma-terials) and improvising. Is it not too much to ask that masters of improvi-sation like Franklin also be models of bureaucratic regularity and efficiency?

---

[51] This insight is that of my colleague Catherine Prelinger. Franklin's foible may also partly account for his blind love for his grandson Temple. See Claude-Anne Lopez and Eugenia W. Herbert, *The Private Franklin: The Man and His Family* (New York: W. W. Norton and Company, 1975), pp. 239–43.

[52] We must be careful, too, not to judge the eighteenth century by our standards. Robert Morris's disregard for the lines between private gain and public good was not atypical, and even John Adams was tolerant of Deane's lax financial ethics. See *Collections of the Massachusetts Historical Society* 73(1925): 76; L. H. Butterfield and Marc Friedlander, eds., *Adams Family Cor-respondence*, 4 vols. to date (Cambridge: The Belknap Press of Harvard University Press, 1963–) 3: 130n; Ferguson, *Power of the Purse*, pp. 71–75.

[53] Butterfield, *Adams Diary and Autobiography*, 3: 37–39.

[54] See John Adams to Elbridge Gerry, 5 December 1778, Wharton, *Revolutionary Diplomatic Correspondence*, 2: 848–50, for evidence that the French distrust extended to all the American mission. Given the American military weakness the French had little reason to confide secrets to the commissioners.

TRANS. AMER. PHIL. SOC.
VOL. 72 PT. 1, 1982

.V. FRANKLIN AND THE FUNCTIONING
OF THE ALLIANCE

For six weeks after the signing of the alliance the commissioners were not officially recognized as representatives of a sovereign nation. France feared a sudden attack by Britain and wished to make a final effort to induce Spain to join the alliance.[1] Franklin used this period to continue his efforts to contact members of Parliament opposed to the North ministry. It appears this was a final attempt to avert a general war by convincing Britain to recognize American independence. In a postscript to a letter to Thomas Walpole on 11 December 1777 Franklin extended his respects to Lords Chatham and Camden, leaders of the Parliamentary opposition. He closed by reminding them that blessed are the peacemakers.[2] The day before the treaties were signed, Franklin told his friend David Hartley that he had delayed "a material operation" in hopes of receiving proposals. Those proposals not forthcoming Franklin concluded, "Therefore adieu my dear friend; and I bid you all *Good Night.*"[3] He continued however until the end of March his attempts to persuade Britain peace was worth the price of American independence.[4] He even sent Jonathan Loring Austin to England to meet with members of the opposition; his orders, committed to memory, apparently were to disabuse them of any hopes that America would settle for terms short of independence.[5]

Franklin's sending of Austin to England was well meaning but highly dangerous. In December 1777 the commissioners had sent Lee's secretary, John Thornton, to meet with the North government about prisoner relief.[6] Thornton's mission aroused the suspicion of the French ambassador in

---

[1] Jonathan R. Dull, *The French Navy and American Independence: A Study of Arms and Diplomacy, 1774-1787* (Princeton: Princeton University Press, 1975), pp. 101-5.

[2] Franklin to Walpole, 11 December 1777 (David Holland, House of Commons Library); the greetings were returned in Walpole to Franklin, 23 December 1777 (APS).

[3] Franklin to Hartley, 5 February 1778 (DLC); emphasis Franklin's.

[4] Franklin to James Hutton, 1-2 February 1778 (AAE); Franklin to David Hartley, 26 February 1778, Albert Henry Smyth, ed., *The Writings of Benjamin Franklin*, 10 vols. (New York: The Macmillan Company, 1907), 7: 109 (note, however, that the postscript of this letter does not appear in either the copy in DLC or the autograph letter signed in NN); Franklin to Hutton, 24 March 1778 (DLC); Franklin to William Pulteney, 30 March 1778 (DLC).

[5] For excerpts from Austin's journal see Edward E. Hale and Edward E. Hale, Jr., eds., *Franklin in France*, 2 vols. (Boston: Roberts Brothers, 1887-1888), 1: 163-64. See also "Memoir of Jonathan Loring Austin," *Boston Monthly Magazine* 2(1826): 57-66; Benjamin Franklin Stevens, ed., *Facsimiles of Manuscripts in European Archives Relating to America, 1775-1783*, 25 vols. (London: privately printed, 1889-1898), 3: no. 340; 22: no. 1906.

[6] See Commissioners to Mr. Thornton, Instructions, 11 December 1777 (DLC). For Thornton as a British agent see above.

Britain, who wondered if it were a cover for negotiation.[7] Vergennes already suspected Lee because of Lee's friendship with Lord Shelburne, the chief disciple of Lord Chatham, advocate of reconciliation with America and war with France; when Vergennes was brought a letter supposedly written by Lee to Shelburne, Lee was totally discredited.[8] Austin dined and perhaps stayed with Shelburne, who also was an old acquaintance of Franklin's. Franklin was lucky to escape Lee's fate.

By the middle of the following March the French court had given up hope of Spanish help for the coming campaign.[9] The French thus were willing to accommodate the commissioners' request that the commercial treaty be made public.[10] As expected, the British recalled their ambassador from Versailles, and both France and Britain began preparing for hostilities. The French court now could acknowledge the commissioners as representatives of a sovereign state. On 20 March they were presented to the king and his council of state and two days later to the royal family.[11]

A few days later Deane, recalled by Congress, left for America.[12] His replacement, John Adams, was greeted by the rumors, all too true, of rancorous animosities and factions in the American mission.[13] With Deane's departure and Lee's hostility Franklin lost his position of informal primacy; by the time of Adam's arrival Lee had come to think of Franklin as corrupt and Franklin to think of Lee as a lunatic.[14] Adams, shocked at the disorder of the commissioners' records, took over the mission's correspondence.[15] In

---

[7] Noailles to Vergennes, 23 December 1777, Henri Doniol, ed., *Histoire de la participation de la France à l'établissement des États-unis d'Amérique*, 5 vols. and supplement (Paris: Imprimerie Nationale, 1886-1898), 2: 655. Of course this may have been deliberate on the commissioners' part.

[8] Ibid., 3: 169n-70n. For French suspicions of Lee see Stevens, *Facsimiles of Manuscripts*, 20: no. 1767; John J. Meng, ed., *Dispatches and Instructions of Conrad Alexander Gérard, 1778-1780* (Baltimore: The Johns Hopkins University Press, 1939), p. 422; Charles Isham, ed., *The Deane Papers* (Collections of the New-York Historical Society, 19-23), 5 vols. (New York: The New-York Historical Society, 1887-1891), 3: 441-43. The letter was counterfeit although Lee did send a letter to Shelburne with Thornton, Francis P. Wharton, ed., *The Revolutionary Diplomatic Correspondence of the United States*, 6 vols. (Washington Government Printing Office, 1889), 2: 450. For Lee's justification of Thornton's missions (he was later sent back to England to gather intelligence) see Edward D. Ingraham, ed., *Papers in Relation to the Case of Silas Deane* (Philadelphia: The Seventy-Six Society, 1855), pp. 161-63; Wharton, *Revolutionary Diplomatic Correspondence*, 2: 679-80.

[9] Dull, *French Navy*, pp. 101-4.

[10] Arthur Lee's Journal, 5 March 1778, Richard Henry Lee, ed., *Life of Arthur Lee, LL.D.*, 2 vols. (Boston: Wells and Lilly, 1829), 1: 399-402.

[11] Ibid., pp. 403-4.

[12] For Deane's recall see Worthington Chauncey Ford et al., eds., *Journals of the Continental Congress, 1774-1789*, 35 vols. (Washington: Library of Congress and National Archives, 1904-1976), 9: 946-47, 975; Isham, *Deane Papers*, 2: 267.

[13] L. H. Butterfield, ed., *Diary and Autobiography of John Adams*, 4 vols. (Cambridge: The Belknap Press of Harvard University Press, 1961), 4: 39-40.

[14] Arthur Lee to Richard Henry Lee, 15 February 1778, R. H. Lee, *Life of Arthur Lee*, 2: 134-35; Arthur Lee to Sam Adams, 17 February 1778, Isham, *Deane Papers*, 2: 368-69, and 22 May 1779, Helen Augur, *The Secret War of Independence* (New York: Duell, Sloan and Pearce, 1955), p. 325; Silas Deane to Jonathan Williams, Jr., 13 January 1778, Isham, *Deane Papers*, 2: 327; Franklin to Lee, 3 April 1778 (APS).

[15] Butterfield, *Adams Diary and Autobiography*, 2: 304-5; 4: 43-44; Wharton, *Revolutionary Diplomatic Correspondence*, 2: 760-61. Adams's claims to have handled all the mission's cor-

spite of his good intentions, though, Adams could do little to alleviate the human disorder within the mission. It was plagued not only by the tension between Lee and Franklin, but also by the presence of the unwanted commissioners to the German powers and Tuscany, William Lee and Ralph Izard. Luckily, William Lee left for Vienna after the French treaties were signed, but Izard, as argumentative as he was intelligent, remained to await an invitation to Florence. Adams, although he professed to be scandalized at Franklin's love of ease and dissipated life, admitted that Arthur Lee and Izard's "Prejudices and violent Tempers would raise Quarrells in the Elisian Fields if not in Heaven."[16] To resolve the impasse, Adams and Lee suggested to Franklin that he go to the Netherlands. Franklin, who did not wish to go, asked Vergennes's advice; Vergennes, who preferred dealing confidentially and individually with Franklin, suggested he stay in France.[17]

The solution came from Congress. France had sent Gérard as minister plenipotentiary to the United States and Congress, forced by diplomatic etiquette to appoint a representative of equal rank, chose Franklin.[18] In February 1779 he received news of his appointment and quickly dismissed his former colleagues.[19]

Although his new life as sole American representative was more peaceful, it was never easy. Aided only by his grandson Temple and at times by an additional secretary, Franklin was so pressed by work he claimed he could not allow himself even a day's excursion in the country. Eventually he complained of the effects on his and Temple's health.[20]

His duties were remarkably varied. Most important, of course, he represented the United States in its dealings with the French government, most often with Vergennes, but occasionally with Naval Ministers Sartine and Castries, War Ministers Montbarey and Ségur, and Finance Ministers Necker and Joly de Fleury.[21] Every Tuesday he attended court with the other foreign representatives. Most of his time, however, was spent in more mundane pursuits, the most onerous of which was cashing American loan office certificates.[22] Franklin also provided services to American warship captains, aided American state agents in their pursuit of matériel or loans

---

respondence are exaggerated. See for example the draft in Franklin's hand of American Commissioners to Jonathan Trumbull, 22 July 1778 (DLC).

[16] Diary entry of 9 February 1779, Butterfield, *Adams Diary and Autobiography*, 2: 346.

[17] Franklin to Vergennes, 20 October 1778 (AAE); Vergennes to Franklin, 21 October 1778 (DLC); Vergennes to Gérard, 25 December 1778, Doniol, *Participation*, 3: 613–15.

[18] For details of Franklin's election (with only Pennsylvania voting against him) see Richard Bache to Franklin, 22 October 1778 (APS).

[19] For Adams's relief at the news see Butterfield, *Adams Diary and Autobiography*, 2: 353–54.

[20] Franklin to Robert R. Livingston, 3 September 1782 (DNA).

[21] Consult Dull, *French Navy and American Independence*, passim.

[22] Franklin had helped bring this chore upon himself; see American Commissioners to Committee of Secret Correspondence, 12 March–9 April 1777 (DNA). Congress, however, also decided to draw bills of exchange on their representatives in Europe: Committee for Foreign Affairs to American Commissioners, 8 November 1777 (ViU); E. James Ferguson, *The Power of the Purse: A History of American Public Finance, 1776–1790* (Chapel Hill: The University of North Carolina Press, 1961), pp. 36–37, 55–56; E. James Ferguson, ed., *The Papers of Robert Morris, 1781–1784*, 5 vols. to date (Pittsburgh: University of Pittsburgh Press, 1973-), 3: 285.

(until the French court objected),[23] issued letters of marque to privateer captains and certified the legitimacy of their captures,[24] inserted articles in the press about American affairs, took oaths of allegiance and issued passports, supervised the purchase and shipping of arms and uniforms, and helped Americans with problems ranging from lost luggage to French admiralty court decrees. His most ardent efforts were devoted to improving the condition of American prisoners of war in Britain and securing their exchange. His correspondents included a member of the royal family (whose groom repeatedly needed passports to bring back hunting dogs from England), noblemen inquiring about relatives serving in America, and scores of commission seekers, poets, sculptors, inventors, amateur genealogists, merchants, manufacturers, beggars and cranks of all types. (My favorite is the Benedictine monk who asked Franklin to pay his gambling debts.)[25] Once a week he entertained his fellow Americans; the other evenings he dined out, generally with the rich or noble who alone could influence the French government.[26] Franklin considered correctly that his chief function should be negotiation and begged for someone to take over the minutiae which so filled his time. He was not reluctant to delegate authority; he had no one to whom he could assign such authority.

Far from finding assistance, Franklin continued to find problems in the presence of other American diplomats and would-be diplomats in Europe. In 1778 William Lee, unwelcome in Berlin and Vienna, had met secretly in Aix-la-Chapelle with a representative of the regents of the city of Amsterdam. Although neither man possessed any real authority, they drafted a treaty of commerce between the United States of America and the United Provinces of the Netherlands. As soon as the commissioners learned of his action they rebuked Lee, but they were too late to undo his meddling.[27] The British in 1780 captured a copy of Lee's draft treaty and used it as an excuse to open hostilities against the Netherlands.[28] After failing to raise a loan for Virginia in the Netherlands, Lee gradually withdrew from public business. He remained in Europe for the rest of the war, however, and periodically pestered Franklin for money.

Ralph Izard had the sense not to go to Florence and, when the invitation was not forthcoming, to request his recall. It was not until 1780 that he returned to the United States; until then his presence was a strain on Franklin's patience and the mission's funds. Arthur Lee, unwelcome in Spain, also returned to the United States in 1780. Like Izard he was elected

---

[23] Franklin to Committee for Foreign Affairs, 26 May 1779 (DLC).

[24] For reasons both of principle and expediency Franklin moved to bring American policy into line with the principle of "free ships, free goods." Franklin to John Torris, 30 May 1780 (APS); to Samuel Huntington, 31 May 1780 (DNA).

[25] Dom Bernard to Franklin, 14 September 1778 (APS).

[26] See Franklin to Margaret Stevenson, 25 January 1779 (DLC).

[27] American Commissioners to Lee, 26 September 1780 (DNA).

[28] A good summary of Lee's action and its consequences is in Samuel Flagg Bemis, *The Diplomacy of the American Revolution*, rev. ed. (Bloomington: Indiana University Press, 1957), pp. 155–61.

to Congress and continued his feud with Franklin from there. John Adams returned to France in early 1780 as Congress's commissioner for negotiating peace as soon as Britain was ready to recognize American independence. Franklin later wrote of Adams, "I am persuaded . . . that he means well for his Country, is always an honest man, often a wise one, but sometimes and in some things, absolutely out of his senses."[29] Certainly Adams's conduct in 1780 was enough to establish such an opinion. At Vergennes's request he reluctantly refrained from communicating his instructions to the British, who, indeed, were far from recognizing American independence. Frustrated by lack of work, Adams compulsively sent prolix dispatches to Congress.[30] Such harmless behavior did not satisfy his Puritan conscience, however. He became involved in a dispute with Vergennes and in a series of insulting dispatches rendered himself virtually persona non grata with the French court. Franklin managed to disavow Adams's conduct while evading support for the French position in the dispute (which largely concerned French dismay at America's devaluating its currency).[31] Adams left for the Netherlands at the end of July in hopes of raising a loan for the United States. When Henry Laurens, Congress's commissioner to the Netherlands, was captured by the British in September, Adams became his replacement.

Adams's two years in the Netherlands were successful, due less to Adams's own efforts than to those of the French ambassador at The Hague. Before Adams returned for the peace negotiations he had secured a commercial treaty and a loan. His delusions of importance were furthered also by the results of the one interruption in his Dutch mission. In the summer of 1781 Adams, still peace commissioner, was summoned by Vergennes. Austria and Russia had offered to mediate the war, and Adams came back to France to help Vergennes formulate a reply on behalf of America. Adams believed that his journey thwarted both the mediation and the machinations of Vergennes to arrange a compromise peace. In fact, Vergennes was opposed to the mediation and was committed to American independence.[32] Adams was justified, however, in seeing Vergennes's hand behind Congress's decision to replace him as single peace commissioner by a body comprised of Adams, Franklin, Henry Laurens, John Jay (the new minister to Spain), and Thomas Jefferson (who arrived well after the completion of peace negotiations). Vergennes had been so appalled at Adams's temperamental instability that he ordered his new minister in the United States, the chevalier de La Luzerne, to lobby for the change.[33]

---

[29] Franklin to Robert R. Livingston, 22–25 July 1783 (DLC).

[30] See Peter Shaw, *The Character of John Adams* (Chapel Hill: University of North Carolina Press, 1976), p. 138.

[31] Franklin to Vergennes, 10 July and 3 August 1780 (AAE); James H. Hutson, *John Adams and the Diplomacy of the American Revolution* (Lexington: The University Press of Kentucky, 1980), pp. 51–74. For Adams's mission to the Netherlands see ibid, pp. 75–116.

[32] Dull, *French Navy*, pp. 211–15.

[33] William C. Stinchcombe, *The American Revolution and the French Alliance* (Syracuse: Syracuse University Press, 1969), pp. 153–69. Gérard had returned to France for reasons of health.

Another American paid a brief visit to Paris in 1781. Congress, distressed by Franklin's failure to obtain greater sums of money, sent Colonel John Laurens, one of Washington's aides, to France with a shopping list of items for the Continental Army. (Ambassador Luzerne told Vergennes that Congress had become convinced by Franklin's failure to write that he was spending little time on public affairs, thereby necessitating Laurens's mission; Luzerne further claimed that only the difficulty of agreeing upon Franklin's successor had kept him from being removed.)[34] When Colonel Laurens arrived, Franklin had just persuaded the French court to promise to grant the United States 6,000,000 livres as a gift.[35] By his blustering Laurens did secure a French promise to guarantee a loan of 10,000,000 livres (5,000,000 guilders) which would be raised in the Netherlands.[36] Unfortunately, before the loan was raised or the grant received, Laurens had ordered millions of livres in specie and military supplies to be sent to the United States. He thus made the immediate financial situation worse rather than better; Franklin was even forced to order 1,500,000 livres in specie disembarked.[37] Moreover, Laurens insisted on sending an agent to purchase the supplies in the Netherlands and consequently alienated the French government. Some of the supplies proved to be British and by American law had to be sold. Finally, the frigate *South Carolina* (the ship built by Boux) left the supply ships behind when she sailed from Amsterdam, thereby stranding them without a convoy escort. This fiasco involved both Franklin and Adams in legal difficulties; in 1782 the newly arrived American consul Thomas Barclay finally was able to clear up the litigation and send the goods to America, but by this time they were no longer needed.[38] Although Laurens had offended Vergennes, he did no permanent harm to Franco-American relations[39]; Franklin, however, was so insulted by Congress's lack of confidence that he asked to resign.[40] When Congress not only refused

---

[34] Luzerne to Vergennes, 15 December 1780, Doniol, *Participation*, 4: 391n; Irving Brant, *James Madison: The Nationalist, 1780–1787* (Indianapolis and New York: The Bobbs-Merrill Company, 1948), pp. 64–66; Stinchcombe, *American Revolution and French Alliance*, p. 140. Franklin had easily survived a recall attempt in 1779. H. James Henderson, "Congressional Factionalism and the Attempt to Recall Benjamin Franklin," *The William and Mary Quarterly*, 3rd ser. 27(1970): 246–67.

[35] This was in addition to 3,000,000 livres in loan already promised. Franklin to Samuel Huntington, President of Congress, 12 March 1781 (DNA). It should be noted that Vergennes had been forewarned of Laurens's mission. Vergennes to Luzerne, 19 February and 8 March 1781, Doniol, *Participation*, 4: 541, 548, 583–88.

[36] John Laurens to the President of Congress, 9 April 1781, Wharton, *Revolutionary Diplomatic Correspondence*, 4: 355–56.

[37] Franklin to Commodore Gillon of the South Carolina Navy, 28 June 1781 (DLC); Franklin to Major William Jackson, 5 July 1781 (DNA).

[38] See John Barry to Franklin, 28 February 1782 (APS); Franklin to Williams, 23 March 1782 (DLC); Ferguson, *Power of the Purse*, pp. 126–27.

[39] Vergennes to Lafayette, 19 April 1781, Stanley J. Idzerda, ed., *Lafayette in the Age of the American Revolution: Selected Letters and Papers, 1776–1790*, 4 vols. to date (Ithaca, N.Y. and London: Cornell University Press, 1977–), 4: 47–48; Vergennes to Luzerne, 11 May 1781, Doniol, *Participation*, 4: 559n–60n.

[40] Franklin to Samuel Huntington, President of Congress, 12 March 1781 (DNA).

his resignation but elected him as one of the peace commissioners, Franklin, his pride assuaged, withdrew the request.[41] Franklin praised Laurens personally,[42] but Lauren's mission at best was a qualified success.

The Americans who remained in Europe after the colonel's departure brought Franklin little more than problems. John Laurens's father, Henry, was a prisoner in London; Franklin volunteered financial aid to him, but it was not needed.[43] Francis Dana, American minister to Russia, went uninvited to St. Petersburg in spite of Franklin's and Vergennes's advice, but other than drawing funds from Franklin on his departure, Dana had little subsequent contact with him.[44] Until 1782 Adams's mission was not self-supporting and Adams repeatedly had to call on Franklin for funds; relations between the two men were distant but proper. (Franklin was solicitous about Adams's health and volunteered his help if Adams wished to send his son John Quincy to Geneva for schooling.)[45] Far warmer were relations between Franklin and John Jay, American minister in Spain. Jay's letters to his colleague in France radiated admiration and friendship, while Franklin expressed the desire to have Jay for his successor and named him executor of his will.[46] In spite of this excellent rapport, Jay chiefly represented for Franklin more demands for money, in large part because of the bills of exchange Congress persisted in drawing upon all its representatives in Europe. Franklin's major problem with his fellow diplomats was the way they compounded his central problem during the years 1779 to 1782, that of procuring the funds necessary for the continuation of the war.

As has happened to other courted virgins, Franklin had become the dependent housewife without independent financial resources or credit.[47] Until 1782 attempts to borrow money from private sources failed. America could not match the interest rates offered by European states and was regarded as an unacceptable credit risk.[48] Franklin thus was thrown back on his ability to coax funds out of the wealthier partner in the alliance. He proved extraordinarily successful. (Franklin, it might be noted, had been

---

[41] Huntington to Franklin, 19 June 1781 (APS); Franklin to Carmichael, 24 August 1781 (DLC); Franklin to Huntington, 13 September 1781 (DNA). For Franklin's continuing desire to retire as soon as it was possible see Franklin to Livingston, 4 March 1782 (DNA).

[42] Franklin to Lafayette, 14 May 1781 (DLC).

[43] Franklin to William Hodgson, 19 November 1781 (MiU-C); Franklin to Sir Grey Cooper, 7 November 1780 (DLC).

[44] The best account of Dana's mission is David M. Griffiths, "American Commercial Diplomacy in Russia, 1780 to 1783," *The William and Mary Quarterly*, 3d ser. 27(1970): 379–410.

[45] Franklin to Adams, 12–16 October 1781 (MHi) and 7 November 1781 (MHi).

[46] Franklin to Jay, 12 April 1781 (DLC). For a history of the warm friendship between the two men (interrupted briefly during the peace negotiations) see Frank Monaghan, *Some Conversations of Dr. Franklin and Mr. Jay* (New Haven: The Three Monks Press, 1936), pp. 1–8.

[47] Franklin did use the analogy of France as husband on at least two occasions. Franklin to David Hartley, 18 February 1778 (MHi) and 16 October 1783 (MiU-C). In the former letter he referred to Britain as a mother-in-law, in the latter as a father. Franklin also spoke of Louis as America's true father. See Franklin to Morris, 25 June 1782 (DLC); Franklin to Vergennes, 8 November 1782 (AAE).

[48] Franklin to Committee for Foreign Affairs, 26 May 1779 (DLC).

married to a marvelously skilled household manager.)[49] His letters to America were full of sound advice: Don't treat France as made of money,[50] don't threaten or appear ungrateful, time your requests according to the way the French governmental budget system functions.[51] Such skill produced results; except for the loan guarantee extracted by Laurens, the French support for the Revolution was Franklin's work. For the years 1779 through 1783 the French loaned the United States 21,000,000 livres, gave 6,000,000 livres and guaranteed another 10,000,000 livres.[52] The bulk of this came in 1781 and averted American financial collapse.

Although financial aid was indispensable, it alone was not sufficient to win the war. The French expeditionary force sent to Newport in 1780 and the French fleet of de Grasse played vital parts in the capture of Cornwallis's army at Yorktown, finally breaking the British will to continue the war in America. Franklin, however, played only a minor part in the French decision to send an expeditionary force to the United States. Lee Kennett, the latest historian of the French in America, speculates that Franklin did not wish to be blamed if the expedition failed.[53] Such caution is not surprising. In proposing the alliance to the commissioners, Gérard had explained that French aid would be only by sea since France supposed it would not be agreeable to the Americans to have foreign troops in their country.[54] In late 1778, however, Congress ordered Franklin to request 4,000 to 5,000 French troops and four ships of the line to help in the capture of Halifax and Quebec.[55] When Franklin forwarded the proposal he instead suggested the French help the United States capture not only Halifax but also Rhode Island, which had been taken by the British at the end of 1776.[56] The idea of sending French forces to Rhode Island was probably that of Franklin's friend Lafayette (who had brought to France the congressional proposals).[57] Franklin let himself be talked into suggesting the idea to Vergennes but he did not tell Congress he had done so,[58] and he left the subsequent lobbying to Lafayette, justifying his abstention by his lack of orders from

[49] Franklin described his tactics in a letter to Samuel Huntington of 9 August 1780 (DNA). Franklin was not above using calculated naiveté. See Franklin to Vergennes, 15–16 February 1782 (AAE), in which he assumed 2,216,000 livres received from the finance minister were in addition to the loans received from the foreign ministry. Vergennes was not deceived. Vergennes to Franklin, 20 February 1782 (DLC); Franklin to Robert Morris, 4 March 1782 (DLC).

[50] For the financial costs of the war to France see Dull, *French Navy and American Independence*, pp. 345–50 and Robert D. Harris, "French Finances and the American War, 1777–1783," *Journal of Modern History* 48(1976): 233–58.

[51] See Franklin to Huntington, 14 May 1781 (DNA); Franklin to Adams, 19 May 1781 (MHi).

[52] Ferguson, *Power of the Purse*, pp. 40–41, 126–28. Counting 1777 and 1778, total French aid was about 47,500,000 livres.

[53] Lee Kennett, *The French Forces in America, 1780–1783* (Westport, Conn.: Greenwood Press, 1977), p. 9.

[54] Arthur Lee's Journal, 8 January 1778, R. H. Lee, *Life of Arthur Lee*, 1: 377.

[55] Ford et al., *Journals of the Continental Congress*, 12: 1039–42.

[56] Franklin to Vergennes, 25 February 1779 (AAE).

[57] See Lafayette to the President of Congress, 29 November 1778, Idzerda, *Lafayette in the Age of the American Revolution*, 2: 205–6; Kennett, *French Forces in America*, pp. 7–9.

[58] Franklin said only that he had recommended the reduction of Halifax and Quebec. Franklin to Committee for Foreign Affairs, 26 May 1779 (DLC).

Congress.[59] Franklin's fear of going beyond his instructions is quite typical, but there are other possible reasons for his reluctance to become directly involved. One is Franklin's diffidence of his knowledge of military affairs.[60] His optimism with regard to eventual American victory was another reason he did not feel it necessary to ask for help. Perhaps most important, he was anxious to minimize the requests he made of Vergennes, particularly when they involved American weakness and dependence on France.[61]

In any case Franklin could not guarantee an American welcome for French troops; it was George Washington's encouragement that removed this last obstacle.[62] The decision to send the expeditionary force, moreover, was made on military grounds; there is no indication that a more active intervention on Franklin's part would have been more effective than Adams's demands that France maintain naval superiority in American waters.[63] Both the expeditionary force and naval superiority involved questions of high strategy which France had to coordinate with Spain, her most important military ally. It is no coincidence that a major role in the decision to reallocate resources to North America was played by the comte de Montmorin, French ambassador to Spain.[64] The fruit of that decision was Yorktown, which would transform Franklin's role once again.

---

[59] Franklin to Lafayette, 1 October 1779 (DLC).

[60] Examples are Franklin to Lafayette, 22 March 1779 (APS); Franklin to Sartine, 1 April 1779 (DLC).

[61] Franklin to Lafayette, 22 March 1779 (APS).

[62] Idzerda, *Lafayette in the Age of the American Revolution*, 2: 313–19, 344–49.

[63] See for example Adams to Vergennes, 13 July 1780 (APS) and 27 July 1780 (PU). Franklin did mention the subject of naval superiority in his letter to Vergennes of 13 February 1781 (AAE).

[64] Dull, *French Navy and American Independence*, pp. 203–6.

Trans. Amer. Phil. Soc.
Vol. 72 Pt. 1, 1982

VI. FRANKLIN THE NEGOTIATOR: SECURING
THE PEACE

As with the case of 1777, we cannot judge Franklin's performance during the years of the alliance merely by analyzing his activities. His greatness as a diplomat lay in his coolness under pressure. Perhaps the best demonstration of this quality was the patience with which he waited for Britain to conclude the war on America's terms. He continued to have sporadic contacts with the British government thoughout the war, but there was no chance of serious negotiation until Britain realized she could not coerce America into acknowledging her sovereignty. The king wrote to North:

> The many instances of the inimical conduct of Franklin towards this country, makes me aware that hatred to this Country is the constant object of his mind. . . . Yet I think it so desirable to end the war with that Country, to be enabled with redoubled ardour to avenge the Faithless and insolent conduct of France that I think it may be proper to keep open the channel of intercourse with the insidious man.[1]

So transparent was George's intention to split the alliance that his emissaries to Franklin in 1778, David Hartley and William Pulteney, stood no chance of success.[2] Franklin not only felt a moral obligation to the French government,[3] but he was almost indescribably bitter toward the North administration, which he described as having hands "red, wet, and dripping with the Blood of my Countrymen, Friends and Relations."[4] On the eve of its fall in March 1782 the North government again attempted to initiate negotiations with Franklin; he turned the correspondence over to the French government.[5]

North's removal from office transformed the diplomatic climate as instantly as had the arrival of news of Saratoga. By chance Franklin had just been presented an opportunity to correspond with his old acquaintance Lord Shelburne, one of the leaders of the opposition.[6] He wrote to thank

---

[1] George III to Lord North, 26 March 1778. Sir John Fortescue, ed., *The Correspondence of King George the Third from 1760 to December 1783*, 6 vols. (London: Macmillan and Company, 1927-1928), 4: 80.

[2] George Herbert Guttridge, *David Hartley, An Advocate of Conciliation, 1774–1783* (Berkeley: University of California Press, 1926), pp. 281–87; Frederick B. Tolles, "Franklin and the Pulteney Mission: An Episode in the Secret History of the American Revolution," *Huntington Library Quarterly* 17(1953): 37–56.

[3] Franklin to Pulteney, 30 March 1778 (DLC); Franklin to Hartley, 4 May 1779 (DLC).

[4] Franklin to James Hutton, 1–12 February 1778, Albert Henry Smyth, ed., *The Writings of Benjamin Franklin*, 10 vols. (New York: The Macmillan Company, 1907), 7: 101.

[5] Franklin to Vergennes's aide, Joseph-Matthias Gérard de Rayneval, 22 March 1782 (AAE).

[6] Franklin's Journal of Negotiations, Carl Van Doren, *Benjamin Franklin's Autobiographical Writings* (New York: Viking Press, 1945), p. 515.

Shelburne for some gooseberry bushes he had sent one of Franklin's neighbors in Passy[7]; the letter reached Shelburne shortly after he had been appointed the colonial secretary of Rockingham's new cabinet. The warmth of Franklin's greetings hardly was coincidence— he had "private advices" of what was occurring in Parliament[8]— and Shelburne quickly responded to the hint. His first steps were to begin action for an exchange of prisoners (the subject nearest to Franklin's heart) and to send to Passy Richard Oswald, a Scots merchant and free-trade advocate who immediately won Franklin's confidence.[9] (Shelburne thereby forestalled his rival, Charles James Fox, foreign secretary in the Rockingham ministry.) Franklin met Oswald in mid-April, 1782, introduced him to Vergennes, and then sent him back to Shelburne with two documents. The first was an official letter expressing a willingness to negotiate, the second a confidential memorandum suggesting as Franklin's own idea that if Shelburne wished a reconciliation and durable peace, Britain should voluntarily cede Canada to the United States. This might in return permit the Loyalists to be compensated for the loss of their estates.[10]

Franklin's suggestion that Britain cede Canada was probably a test of the sincerity of Shelburne's liberal views both on reconciliation with America and on the pointlessness of Britain's retaining colonies. Of particular interest is the fact that Franklin made the suggestion in confidence. Four years earlier he had stated to an English friend that for the sake of a lasting and profitable peace, Britain should not only drop her pretensions to govern the United States but should also cede Canada, Nova Scotia, and Florida as indemnification for the burning of American towns.[11] He had given a copy of that letter to the French foreign ministry. Since then, Franklin as a prospective peace commissioner had been ordered by Congress

to make the most candid and confidential communications upon all subjects to the ministers of our generous ally, the King of France; to undertake nothing in the negotiations for peace or truce without their knowledge and concurrence; and ultimately to govern [himself] by their advice and opinion. . . .[12]

Jay objected bitterly to these instructions. Franklin praised them wholeheartedly yet disregarded them as soon as negotiations began.[13]

---

[7] Franklin to Shelburne, 22 March 1782 (PRO).

[8] Franklin to Livingston, 9 March 1782 (DNA).

[9] Shelburne to Franklin, 6 April 1782 (PRO); William Hodgson to Franklin, 9 April 1782 (APS).

[10] Franklin's Journal, Van Doren, *Autobiographical Writings*, pp. 516–23 (note that the dates in Franklin's Journal are not to be relied upon); Richard Oswald's Journal, 7–19 April 1782 (PRO); Franklin to Shelburne, 18 April 1782 (PRO); Franklin, Memorandum given to Oswald [18 April 1782] (DLC).

[11] Franklin to James Hutton, 1–12 February 1778 (AAE).

[12] Instructions . . ., 15 July 1781, Worthington Chauncey Ford et al., eds., *Journals of the Continental Congress, 1774–1789*, 35 vols. (Washington: Library of Congress and National Archives, 1904–1976), 20: 651, 652.

[13] Jay to President of Congress [Huntington], 21 September 1781, Francis P. Wharton, ed., *The Revolutionary Diplomatic Correspondence of the United States*, 6 vols. (Washington Government Printing Office, 1889), 4: 716–18; Franklin to Huntington, 13 September 1781 (DNA). Privately Franklin did tell Jay he agreed with him about the instructions, Franklin to Jay, 19 January 1782 (NNC).

There is further evidence of Franklin's intentions. Just before the start of the negotiations, he received instructions from Robert R. Livingston, the recently appointed American secretary for foreign affairs. Livingston urged a firm stand on western boundaries, American fishing rights, and no compensation for Loyalists.[14] Franklin replied:

Your Communication of the Sentiments of Congress with Regard to many Points that may come under Consideration in a Treaty of Peace, gives me great Pleasure and the more as they agree so perfectly with my own Opinions and furnish me with additional Arguments in their Support.[15]

He had already told Jay that he would prefer buying at a great price the right to navigate the Mississippi to selling a drop of its waters: "A Neighbour might as well ask me to sell my Street Door."[16] From such comments it is obvious Franklin was likely to be a tough and uncompromising negotiator; from the secrecy of the memorandum sent with Oswald it is equally obvious he would not let himself be restricted by France.

Franklin's proposal to Shelburne, however, was an inauspicious beginning for the negotiations. The recommendation was not only unrealistic in terms of what Shelburne was free to offer, but also was very imprudent. It was quickly rebuffed; indeed, Franklin was fortunate Shelburne was honorable enough not to reveal to the French the American suggestion. Particularly unfortunate was the hint about the Loyalists, a hint which Franklin soon claimed to regret and which raised false British expectations of American flexibility.

The British cabinet responded to Franklin's official letter by ordering Oswald back to Passy to negotiate. Although Shelburne kept Franklin's proposal a secret even from his colleagues, his own instructions to Oswald offered no hope that the United States would be given Canada.[17] The cabinet also authorized Fox to name a representative to negotiate with Vergennes. Fox chose Thomas Grenville, a reliable political ally, but only twenty-six years old and like Oswald without prior diplomatic experience.[18] Meanwhile, Franklin had written to his fellow peace commissioners Adams,

[14] Livingston to Franklin, 7 January 1782 (DNA). Two weeks later Congress resolved that the peace commissioners should earnestly contend for the first two objects, Ford et al., *Journals of the Continental Congress*, 22: 44–45.

[15] Franklin to Livingston, 9 March 1782 (DNA); cf. Franklin to Livingston, 30 March 1782 (DNA).

[16] Franklin to Jay, 2 October 1780, Albert Henry Smyth, ed., *The Writings of Benjamin Franklin*, 10 vols. (New York: The Macmillan Company, 1907), 8: 144. For Franklin's fears that Spain wished to shut the United States within the Appalachians see Franklin to Livingston, 12 April 1782 (DNA).

[17] Minutes of cabinet enclosed with Shelburne to George III, 26 April 1782, Fortescue, *Correspondence of King George the Third*, 5: 488; Richard B. Morris, *The Peacemakers: The Great Powers and American Independence* (New York: Harper & Row, 1965), pp. 269–71; Vincent T. Harlow, *The Founding of the Second British Empire*, Volume One: *Discovery and Revolution* (London: Longmans, Green and Company, 1952), p. 251.

[18] Shelburne to Franklin, 28 April 1782 (DLC). In theory Oswald's mission was merely to negotiate the preliminaries of the time and place for subsequent negotiations. In practice the king wished Oswald in France as a check on the negotiations being conducted by Fox, whom the king intensely distrusted. George III to Shelburne, 27 April 1782, Fortescue, *Correspondence of King George the Third*, 5: 494.

Laurèns, and Jay to come join him.[19] Adams, involved in negotiating a commercial treaty with the Dutch, refused[20]; Laurens, although now free on parole, also refused.[21] Jay accepted, but he had to finish business in Madrid before leaving the American mission to his secretary, William Carmichael. Jay did not arrive until 23 June and then was incapacitated by influenza. The preliminary stages of the peace negotiation thus were left to Franklin. Luckily, France did not insist upon being consulted. Vergennes soon told Franklin that the king wished the Americans to treat for themselves and make their own treaty, provided that all treaties went hand in hand and were signed the same day.[22]

The situation was perfect for Franklin's particular diplomatic skills, those of ambiguity and patient waiting. The task he faced called for all the delicacy at his disposal. On the one hand he hinted to Oswald and Grenville that in return for British recognition of American independence America would assist Britain in her endeavors to make a reasonable peace with France.[23] On the other hand he was obviously aware that America was still dependent on France for financial aid and, if negotiations broke down, for military aid in driving the British from New York and Charleston. He therefore could not say anything explicit to Grenville or Oswald for fear of jeopardizing French confidence in America's continued loyalty to the alliance. In mid-July Franklin spoke to Vergennes's undersecretary Joseph-Mathias Gérard de Rayneval of his conversations with Oswald and Grenville and suggested a mutual agreement that a subsequent British attack on any signatory to a general peace would be considered an attack on them all.[24] He was even able to obtain from Vergennes the remission of prior interest owed on French loans to the United States and a staggered repayment schedule for the principal and subsequent interest.[25]

Franklin's astuteness is most clearly shown by his fostering his contacts with Shelburne's representative, Oswald, instead of abandoning Oswald in order to deal with Fox's man, Grenville.[26] Fox, unlike Shelburne, favored immediate British recognition of American independence, expecting America then to reach agreement quickly with Britain on the other peace terms

[19] Franklin to Adams, 20 April 1782 (MHi); Franklin to Henry Laurens, 20 April 1782 (ScHi); Franklin to John Jay, 22 April 1782 (Royal Library, Windsor).

[20] Adams to Franklin, 2 May 1782 (MHi); for speculations on the psychological dimension of Adams's refusal see Peter Shaw, *The Character of John Adams*, (Chapel Hill: University of North Carolina Press, 1976), p. 162; James H. Hutson, "John Adams and the Diplomacy of the American Revolution" (Ph.D. diss. Yale University, 1964), pp. 146, 153–54.

[21] Laurens to Franklin, 17 May 1782, Van Doren, *Autobiographical Writings*, pp. 545–47.

[22] Franklin's Journal, 29 May 1782, ibid., p. 553.

[23] Grenville to Fox, 10 and 17 May 1782, Lord John Russell, ed., *Memoirs and Correspondence of Charles James Fox*, 4 vols. (London: Richard Bentley, 1853–1857), 4: 180–91; Fox to George III, 21 May 1782, Fortescue, *Correspondence of King George the Third*, 6: 41. Compare these to Franklin's own account, Van Doren, *Autobiographical Writings*, pp. 541–42. My assessment follows that of Harlow, *Second British Empire*, pp. 238–47.

[24] Franklin's Journal, 11 June 1782, Van Doren, *Autobiographical Writings*, p. 570. For Franklin's solicitude about maintaining good relations with Vergennes see the entry for 28 June, ibid., p. 583.

[25] Franklin to Robert Morris, 25 June 1782 (DLC).

[26] See Franklin to Shelburne, 13 May 1782 (PRO).

and drop out of the alliance.[27] Fox hoped then to create an alliance of Britain, Prussia, and Russia to crush France and Spain.[28] Franklin was wise not to be enticed by Fox, who needed the king's consent to his plans; in a bitter series of cabinet battles, Fox's plan for prior recognition of American independence was defeated.[29] On 1 July Rockingham died and Shelburne soon assumed control of the government as first lord of the treasury; Fox's resignation as foreign secretary was anticlimactic. By refusing to rise to Fox's hints, Franklin had preserved his standing with both Shelburne and Vergennes and could continue to play the two against each other.[30]

Franklin and Shelburne thus far had played a waiting game. Shelburne hoped for some concession from Franklin which would preserve some link between Britain and America or would put pressure on France. Franklin, confident of ultimate victory, waited for Shelburne to concede in principle on independence. Upon learning of Shelburne's new appointment, Franklin notified him that he expected an "acknowledgment" of American independence before he would listen to proposals and informed Shelburne of what terms would be necessary to obtain peace. He hinted that if proper terms were granted there might eventually be a federal union between Britain and the United States (presumably a commercial union); if not, the United States might be driven "into the hands of other people."[31] Franklin was so imperturbable that he found time to send his friend Jan Ingenhousz a twenty-page letter on the effects of lightning.[32] Such toughness and patience finally prevailed. Shelburne, anxious for peace to bolster his political position and to inaugurate domestic reforms, finally became convinced that Franklin would settle for nothing short of independence. In late July he issued Oswald a commission to treat and conclude a peace and promised to make independence "the basis and preliminary of the treaty." He also promised to accept as a basis for negotiation Franklin's position on territorial boundaries and American fishing rights.[33]

---

[27] See Fox's informal instructions to Grenville, 30 April 1782, Russell, *Charles James Fox*, pp. 174–78; Fox to Grenville, 21 and 26 May 1782, ibid., pp. 191–99, 206–9.

[28] Isabel de Madariaga, *Britain, Russia and the Armed Neutrality of 1780; Sir James Harris's Mission to St. Petersburg during the American Revolution* (New Haven and London: Yale University Press, 1962), pp. 387–92.

[29] Harlow, *Second British Empire*, pp. 251–63.

[30] Franklin's stated reasons for preferring to deal with Oswald were based on Oswald's character and knowledge of America. Franklin's Journal, 3 June 1782, Van Doren, *Autobiographical Writings*, p. 564. One suspects this does not cover the case. Fox and Grenville subsequently undercut their position with Franklin by leaking to the press Franklin's hints; ibid., pp. 566–67.

[31] Oswald to Shelburne, 10 July 1782, Russell, *Charles James Fox*, pp. 239–44; Franklin to Benjamin Vaughan, 11 July 1782 (APS: typescript); Franklin to Oswald, 12 July 1782 (PRO).

[32] Franklin to Ingenhousz, 21 June 1782 (DLC).

[33] Shelburne to Oswald, 27 July 1782, Lord Esmond Fitzmaurice, *Life of William, Earl of Shelburne, afterwards first Marquess of Landsdowne*, 3 vols. (London: Macmillan and Company, 1876), 3: 246–50. For Oswald's commission of 25 July and instructions of 31 July see Russell, *Charles James Fox*, pp. 262–65, 267–73. Shelburne also sent a personal representative, Franklin's editor, Benjamin Vaughan, to assure Franklin of his good intentions and entrusted Vaughan with extracts from his correspondence with the British commanders in America. Franklin had the ill grace to leak the correspondence to Vergennes. Franklin to Vergennes, 24 July 1782 (AAE); Vaughan to Shelburne, 31 July 1782 (APS); Harlow, *Second British Empire*, pp. 268–73 has an excellent discussion of these developments.

Peace on Franklin's terms seemingly was within grasp. On the apparent eve of victory, however, Jay finally entered the negotiations. Franklin was willing to accept Oswald's commission as a sufficient basis for negotiation and to wait for formal recognition until the completion of an agreement. (Apparently Franklin was ready from the first to strike a separate agreement contingent upon a general peace, thereby putting pressure on the French to settle with Britain.) Jay, less confident, wished an explicit acknowledgment of American independence in case negotiations subsequently broke down. He therefore refused to accept Oswald's commission because it did not mention the United States by name.[34] On this key issue, Franklin, who hated contestation, gave in to Jay.[35] Shortly thereafter, Franklin was incapacitated by an attack of kidney stone so severe he feared for his life.[36]

Jay now took control of the negotiations. In spite of the patience and negotiating skill he had shown in Spain, he lacked Franklin's finesse, and more important, Franklin's iron nerves. He began by putting pressure on Shelburne that was no longer needed.[37] Gradually, however, as he became certain that France was trying secretly to strike a deal with Britain at America's expense, he lost his nerve. I shall discuss shortly the legitimacy of Jay's fears (which were based in part on information leaked by the British); these suspicions convinced Jay that since France was not to be trusted, it was all the more vital to secure British recognition of American independence. Jay therefore proposed that in exchange for a recognition of independence and favorable terms on the fisheries and boundaries, the United States would abandon the French alliance.[38] Jay (this time with Franklin's concurrence) then accepted a compromise on the wording of Oswald's commission by which the United States would be mentioned by name. Finally in mid-September, Jay, by now in near panic, secretly sent an agent to England to offer a separate peace.[39] At the beginning of October serious negotiations were finally established. The change in Oswald's commission had been purchased by seven weeks' delay.[40] Just as negotiations

---

[34] Richard Oswald: Conversations with Franklin and Jay, 7–17 August 1782, Richard B. Morris, ed., *John Jay: The Winning of the Peace—Unpublished Papers 1780–1784* (New York: Harper & Row, 1980), pp. 286–309; Franklin to Rayneval, 4 September 1782 (AAE). For another explanation of Jay's motives see Morris, *John Jay*, p. 309n.

[35] Apparently this happened between the 11 August meeting of Franklin and Oswald and 14 August when the first negotiating session was canceled. Oswald to Townshend, the British colonial secretary, 13–15 August and 17 August 1782 (PRO); see also Franklin to Jay, 16 August 1782 (APS).

[36] The attack was also accompanied by sciatica and by an attack of gout in his legs and thighs. Herbert E. Klingelhofer, "Matthew Ridley's Diary during the Peace Negotiations of 1782," *William and Mary Quarterly*, 3d ser. 20(1963): 101 (entry of 28 August 1782); memorandum of Richard Oswald on the obverse of a letter of David Hartley's, 8 September 1782 (MiU-C); Franklin to Henry Laurens (?), 17 September 1782. As late as 8 January 1783 Franklin reported he still had trouble going up and down stairs, Franklin to Mary Hewson (APS).

[37] And which according to Harlow, *Second British Empire*, p. 277, merely stiffened the backs of the British.

[38] Harlow, *Second British Empire*, pp. 279–85.

[39] This was Benjamin Vaughan, who had remained in Paris after making contact with Franklin.

[40] For Franklin's criticism of the delay see Klingelhofer, "Matthew Ridley's Diary," pp. 111–12 (entry of 21 September 1782); for Jay's acting behind Franklin's back see ibid., pp. 113–14.

began, news arrived of a major British victory at Gibraltar. The opinion of king and public had hardened against concessions and at the reopening of Parliament scheduled for the end of November, Shelburne's hands would be tied. Only by confirming the king in his conviction that the Royal Navy was disintegrating had Shelburne maintained the momentum of negotiations.[41] Thanks to Jay's delay, the final negotiations would require all the time Shelburne had left.

Because of Franklin's continued ill health the first few days of serious negotiation were handled by Jay, who thus was given the chance for a final act of rashness. In order to undercut Spanish claims to the Mississippi Valley, he seconded Oswald's suggestion to his superiors that the British reconquer West Florida from Spain.[42] (Although the idea was rejected, the preliminary agreement did contain a secret clause giving expanded borders to Florida if it were British.) This, however, was Jay's last independent act. Within a few days he was joined by Franklin and on 26 October by John Adams; even Henry Laurens arrived to participate in the final negotiating sessions on 29 November.[43]

The last stage of negotiations was marked by a high degree of unity among the American peace commissioners. The only issue dividing them was Franklin's suggestion that they keep Vergennes informed. This motion was voted down by Jay and Adams, actions it may be assumed Franklin fully expected.[44] (On another issue—Jay's proposal that Britain attack Florida—Franklin's position is ambiguous; although he supported the secret clause, he and Adams refused to agree to permit British troops in New York free passage to carry out the expedition.)[45] The commissioners' unanimity was very fortunate. Shelburne was desperate to obtain a peace settlement before the reconvening of Parliament on 26 November (postponed at the last moment to 5 December). He therefore was willing to yield to American wishes regarding boundaries and fishing rights. The com-

---

[41] See Shelburne to George III, 15 September 1782, Fortescue, *Correspondence of King George the Third*, 6: 127–29. Shelburne's pessimistic appraisal of the condition of the British navy is highly suspect. It differs markedly from the opinion of Viscount Keppel, the first lord of the admiralty, from that of such fleet commanders as Samuel Hood, and from that of Vergennes. See Piers Mackesy, *The War for America, 1775–1783* (Cambridge: Harvard University Press, 1964), pp. 516–17.

[42] Oswald to Townshend, 2 October 1782 (PRO). Jay's draft treaty of 5 October also made significant and perhaps unnecessary concessions with regard to fishing rights and the northeast boundary question. Hutson, *John Adams and the Diplomacy of the American Revolution* (Lexington: The University Press of Kentucky, 1980), pp. 124–25.

[43] Jay to Livingston, 12 December 1782, Wharton, *Revolutionary Diplomatic Correspondence*, 6: 130. There are detailed discussions of the final negotiations in Hutson, *John Adams and the Diplomacy of the American Revolution*, pp. 118–28 and Morris, *The Peacemakers*, pp. 341–85.

[44] John Adams to Mercy Warren, 8 August 1807, *Collections of the Massachusetts Historical Society*, 5th ser. 4(1878): 427–28; John Adams to the *Boston Patriot*, 11 August 1811, Charles Francis Adams, ed., *The Works of John Adams, Second President of the United States, with a Life of the Author*, 10 vols. (Boston: Little, Brown and Company, 1856), 1: 669–74. For the success of Franklin's tactics in avoiding blame see Vergennes to Luzerne, 19 December 1782, Henri Doniol, ed., *Histoire de la participation de la France à l'établissement des États-unis d'Amérique*, 5 vols. and supplement (Paris: Imprimerie Nationale, 1886–1898), 5: 194.

[45] Morris, *The Peacemakers*, p. 346; see also Adams to Livingston, 6 November 1782, Wharton, *Revolutionary Diplomatic Correspondence*, 5: 857–58.

missioners had to procure the maximum number of concessions while not pushing Shelburne so hard that he would break off the negotiations in order to strike a deal with France and Spain. The key issue was that of compensation for the Loyalists, which Shelburne needed for his political survival.[46] At the last moment the commissioners agreed to recommend to the states restitution for British subjects and Loyalists. This face-saving gesture was accompanied by a warning from Franklin that pushing the issue further would result in American claims for compensation from Britain for war damages.[47]

The Loyalist concession was enough to win the agreement; on 30 November the two parties signed a preliminary peace settlement conditional upon a general agreement being reached by the other belligerents. The Americans' concessions, however, were not enough to save Shelburne's ministry. Though Parliament was unwilling to reject Shelburne's agreements, it finally denied him a vote of confidence in February 1783, causing his resignation.[48] Shelburne was a sincere advocate of Anglo-American reconciliation, and the survival of his ministry might have mitigated the generation's worth of bad relations between Britain and the United States which culminated in the War of 1812. It is difficult, however, to see how Shelburne's fall could have been avoided. Shelburne's desire for cooperation with an independent United States was as advanced for its time as was his desire for friendly relations with France[49]; neither policy had a constituency, so both depended on Shelburne's limited ability to manipulate Parliament. As it was, the commissioners went well beyond their instructions concerning the Loyalists,[50] and they expected to be reprimanded.[51] It is difficult to see how they could have conceded enough to save Shelburne, even had they been able to see better the usefulness of making the effort.

The commissioners' immediate problem after the signing was placating France, upon whom America was still financially dependent. Although the agreement was provisional in nature, this was a jesuitical evasion of Congress's instructions "to undertake nothing in the negotiations for peace or truce without their [the French ministers'] knowledge and concurrence." With marvelous tact Franklin apologized to Vergennes for the commissioners' "neglecting a point of bienséance" and expressed their hope that

---

[46] John Norris, *Shelburne and Reform* (London: Macmillan and Company, 1963), pp. 257–58.

[47] Franklin: Proposed Article, 29 November 1782 (APS); Franklin to Oswald, 26 October 1782 (MiU-C); L. H. Butterfield, ed., *Diary and Autobiography of John Adams*, 4 vols. (Cambridge: The Belknap Press of Harvard University Press, 1961), 3: 79–81. Adams believed Franklin more hostile to the Loyalists than was either he or Jay, ibid., p. 77; this of course can be explained on personal grounds since Franklin's son William was a Loyalist.

[48] Norris, *Shelburne and Reform*, pp. 240–70.

[49] Harlow, *Second British Empire*, p. 228.

[50] "The restoration of confiscated property has become utterly impossible, and the attempt would throw the Country into the utmost confusion," Livingston to Franklin, 9 August 1782 (DNA); see also Livingston to Franklin, 7 January 1782 (DNA); Ford et al., *Journals of the Continental Congress*, 18: 948–50; 20: 746–47; 23: 562–63.

[51] Franklin confessed to Livingston on 4 December, "We may have yielded too much in favour of the Royalists" (DNA). See also Vaughan to Shelburne, 4 December 1782, *Proceedings of the Massachusetts Historical Society*, 2d ser. 17(1903): 421–23.

the great work so nearly brought to perfection "not be ruined by a single indiscretion of ours."[52] Franklin's apology was fortunately timed. On the preceding day Spanish Ambassador Aranda had agreed to a new compromise on terms which, if ratified by King Charles III, promised an end to the war.[53] The outcome, however, was still uncertain, and if the war continued France would need at least a nominal American presence to tie down British troops. Franklin thus was able not only to appease Vergennes but also to obtain the promise of another 6,000,000 livre loan to the United States.[54]

Fox six weeks after the signing of their agreement the commissioners waited in almost total ignorance of the progress of the remaining negotiations. On 18 January they were asked to come to Versailles at 10:00 A.M. on the 20th for a matter very interesting to the United States.[55] On that day a general armistice was signed. Ironically, the lack of prior warning prevented Franklin from fulfilling a promise which, although unethical, speaks of his humanity. Long ago he had guaranteed advance knowledge of the results of the negotiations to William Hodgson, the British merchant who had been his chief medium for providing assistance to American prisoners of war in England.[56] Franklin, to his regret, could not carry out his responsibility to Hodgson; he made no attempt to give any information to his own grandnephew Jonathan Williams, Jr. (although Temple Franklin apparently did so).[57] As it happened, the only person to whom he gave advanced knowledge was Captain Joshua Barney of the packet *Washington*, who was waiting to carry the preliminary agreement to America as soon as a general armistice was signed.[58]

The commissioners hoped to obtain further concessions from Britain during the negotiations for a definitive peace treaty. Such hopes were doomed by the hostility of British public opinion.[59] The final treaty, which was signed on 3 September 1783, did not differ substantially from the agreement signed the preceding November 30.

Historians ever since have argued the merits of Jay's and Franklin's ap-

---

[52] Franklin to Vergennes, 17 December 1782, Smyth, *Writings of Franklin*, 8: 643.

[53] Jonathan R. Dull, *The French Navy and American Independence: A Study of Arms and Diplomacy, 1774–1787* (Princeton: Princeton University Press, 1975), pp. 329–32.

[54] Vergennes to Franklin, 19 December 1782 (DLC); Vergennes to Luzerne, 19 and 21 December 1782, Doniol, *Participation* 4: 192–94, 197–98; Franklin to Morris, 20 December 1782 (Ct). The commissioners' action did have its welcome side, that of increasing pressure on Spain to reach agreement, and Vergennes chose to give a favorable interpretation to it: Vergennes to Rayneval, 30 December 1782 (AAE).

[55] Vergennes to Franklin, 18 January 1783 (DLC); since Laurens and Jay were not present, Adams and Franklin had to represent the United States.

[56] See Hodgson to Franklin, 20 March 1781 (APS); Franklin to Hodgson, 1 April 1781 (APS); Hodgson to Franklin 8 May 1781 (APS), etc.

[57] Franklin to Hodgson, 14 January 1783 (APS); Williams to William Temple Franklin, 20 December 1782 (APS).

[58] He was notified so he would not purchase wartime insurance for any goods he was carrying on his own account. Franklin to Barney, 5 December 1782 (Md-An).

[59] Hutson, "John Adams and the Diplomacy of the American Revolution," pp. 171–77; Morris, *The Peacemakers*, pp. 425–37.

proaches to the peace negotiations.[60] Much of the debate has hinged on whether the commissioners should have more fully trusted Vergennes, as Franklin's defenders have claimed, or whether Jay's fears of French duplicity were justified. The debate in more than one sense has been academic; I suspect that Franklin would not have advocated informing Vergennes about the details of the negotiations had he not known he would be outvoted by Adams and Jay. Nonetheless, Franklin's defense of Vergennes's integrity almost certainly was sincere and his debate with Adams and Jay over French motives genuine.[61]

The French records do not provide a simple resolution of the debate. Vergennes was neither the honest broker Congress wished nor the hostile betrayer Jay and Adams believed. Instead he was a man obsessed by France's need for peace, needed because the French navy was crumbling, the financial resources of the government were exhausted, and there was a growing danger of a major war in eastern Europe.[62] Jay's interpretation of Vergennes's motives was erroneous. Vergennes's encouragement of the commissioners to accept Oswald's original commission, his attempts to mediate the rival Spanish and American claims to the area west of the Appalachians, and his sending Rayneval to England to meet Shelburne were all designed chiefly to speed a peace agreement rather than to harm American interests. Jay's delay of the peace negotiations seems all the more irresponsible, given the fact France stood little chance of successfully fighting another campaign.

Although Franklin also did not understand the precise reasons, he realized France's need for peace.[63] His benign view of Vergennes's intentions needs qualification, however. The overpowering French need for peace had two edges when it came to American interests. On one side it meant that Vergennes was perfectly willing to let Franklin and his colleagues negotiate their own treaty, as long as they did not delay the conclusion of a general treaty among the combatants. (This display of faith provides considerable backing for the view that Vergennes's primary motive in lobbying Congress to place Adams under his control was fear that Adams's instability would endanger any peace negotiations.)[64] Moreover, the extremity of France's

---

[60] The most eloquent justification of Jay is probably Morris, *The Peacemakers*; for Franklin, Irving Brant, *James Madison: The Nationalist, 1780–1787* (Indianapolis and New York: The Bobbs-Merrill Company, 1948).

[61] Klingelhofer, "Matthew Ridley's Diary," pp. 106–8; Hutson, "John Adams and the Diplomacy of the American Revolution," pp. 144–46; Jay to Livingston, 18 September 1782, Wharton, *Revolutionary Diplomatic Correspondence* 5: 740.

[62] These conditions are described in detail in Dull, *French Navy and American Independence*, pp. 297–302.

[63] See Franklin to Livingston, 22–25 July 1783 (DLC). On 9 June 1782 Franklin had recorded his own suspicions that Austria and Russia might be intending to drive the Turks from Europe. There is no indication, however, that he realized the enormous importance to Vergennes of this danger to a critical French ally. Van Doren, *Autobiographical Writings*, p. 568. John Adams was no more aware; see Adams to Francis Dana, 17 September 1782, Wharton, *Revolutionary Diplomatic Correspondence*, 5: 732.

[64] Vergennes to Luzerne, 19 February and 19 April 1781, Doniol, *Participation*, 4: 583–84, 588–90.

need for peace reduced to a secondary consideration any intrinsic French interest in such issues as the disposition of the American West, the navigation of the Mississippi, and American fishing rights in *British* fishing grounds off North America.[65] On the other side, however, it meant Vergennes was not likely to be very solicitous about American interests beyond the essential goal of the alliance: the independence and territorial integrity of the settled parts of the thirteen states. Vergennes's views on the area to the west of the Appalachians was clear-cut and supremely logical: since the area was virtually unoccupied except by Indians, its future would have to be negotiated by Britain, the United States, and Spain in relation to what they would be willing to trade.[66] Spain was never really in the bidding. She had too few bargaining chips (West Florida, Minorca, the Bahamas) and too many desires (such as Gibraltar and Jamaica) which were more important to her than the area in question. Britain held a strong overall bargaining position and did possess Detroit, the major military post in the West. Britain's difficulty was that the West was of little value economically without an outlet to the sea, and Spain was unwilling to part with New Orleans. Had Spain been willing, Vergennes would gladly have seen the American West *and* New Orleans given to Britain and an equivalent given to Spain.[67] When this fell through, the West lost its importance to Vergennes and Shelburne proved willing to let it go to the Americans. The Americans also claimed a right to navigation of the Mississippi, though the Spanish held both banks for hundreds of miles from its mouth. The victorious British had won such a concession in 1763; one cannot fault Vergennes for not taking seriously the Americans' demand for comparable treatment.

The American commissioners' action in signing a conditional agreement was a violation of the spirit, if not the letter, of their instructions. It is difficult to blame them. Vergennes could hardly have given his approval had he been asked; as it was, the news of the conditional agreement led to the quick disintegration of the Continental Army in March 1783.[68] Moreover, the news of the American agreement undermined an enormously complicated system of territorial exchanges among Britain, France, and Spain designed to secure Spanish agreement to terms; the British cabinet and public were hardly willing to bribe both Spain and the United States. It thus was fortunate the Americans reached agreement first, forcing the other belligerents to renegotiate *their* terms. If one can excuse the commissioners for the failure of "bienséance," as Franklin had delicately put

---

[65] On the last point see Orville T. Murphy, "The Comte de Vergennes, the Newfoundland Fisheries and the Peace Negotiations of 1783; A Reappraisal," *Canadian Historical Review* 46(1965): 32–46. Probably the French would have preferred the British retain the West (as they did Canada) so as to perpetuate American dependence on the French alliance. Vergennes described the advantages to Spain of this: Vergennes to Montmorin, 6 October 1782 (AAE).

[66] See Jay's informative letter to Livingston of 17 November 1782, Wharton, *Revolutionary Diplomatic Correspondence*, pp. 23–27.

[67] Dull, *French Navy and American Independence*, p. 328. The possibility of the exchange was first raised by Shelburne (during his meeting of 13 September with Rayneval).

[68] E. James Ferguson, *The Power of the Purse: A History of American Public Finance, 1776–1790* (Chapel Hill: The University of North Carolina Press, 1961), pp. 168–69.

it, the same is not true for their inducing Britain to attack Spanish-held Florida. By encouraging Britain to take Florida, the commissioners increased the danger that Britain would also seek to retain the American West. Even without this happening, the reconquest of Florida by Britain would likely have had drastic consequences for American history, particularly in strengthening Britain's bonds with the slave-holding American South. Luckily, the British, for logistical reasons, rejected the idea,[69] and the French did not learn of it until after the armistice. Not only was the proposal foolish, it was highly dishonorable—Spain not only had provided money and matériel to the United States, but her navy had played a vital role in the winning of the war.[70] The American commissioners' encouraging a mutual enemy to attack her was a poor omen for the diplomatic future of a supposedly peace-loving and friendly nation.

It is difficult to speculate what Franklin would have done had a general agreement fallen through. As William Stinchcombe points out, the news of the provisional agreement was generally regarded in America as the end of the war, and the news of the general armistice (which arrived two weeks later) was anticlimactic.[71] Congress had promised to prosecute the war with vigor until a general peace was obtained[72], but it is unlikely many would have listened. The British would have been left the options of retaining impregnable bases in New York and Charleston or of using the garrisons to capture the French West Indies. Jay certainly would have been opposed to American continuation in the war[73]; Franklin's comments on the subject were ambiguous and enigmatic.[74] Luckily for Franklin, he was not forced to choose between the two objects of his diplomacy—the alliance and the peace. His contributions to both remain his finest accomplishment as a diplomat.

---

[69] See also Harlow, *Second British Empire*, pp. 304–8.

[70] Dull, *French Navy and American Independence*, passim. Few but Madison seem to have been aware of Spain's military contribution. Brant, *James Madison*, pp. 278–79. There is a brief mention of Spanish assistance in Franklin's Journal of the Peace Negotiations, Van Doren, *Autobiographical Writings*, p. 557.

[71] William C. Stinchcombe, *The American Revolution and the French Alliance* (Syracuse: Syracuse University Press, 1969), pp. 195–99.

[72] See the congressional resolution of 3 October 1782, Ford, et al., *Journals of the Continental Congress*, 23: 632–37.

[73] Oswald to Townshend, 2 October 1782 (PRO); Grantham to George III, 3 November 1782, Fortescue, *Correspondence of King George the Third*, 6: 150.

[74] Compare Franklin to Hartley, 16 February 1782 (DLC; copy in AAE); Franklin to Hartley, 2 February 1780 (DLC); Franklin's Journal of Negotiations, 1 June 1782, Van Doren, *Autobiographical Writings*, pp. 556–57.

TRANS. AMER. PHIL. SOC.
VOL. 72 PT. 1, 1982

VII. FRANKLIN: DIPLOMAT AND MAN

On returning from his first mission to France, Adams wrote the president of Congress concerning his former colleague:

I presume Congress intends to appoint a secretary to the commission, and to appoint consuls for the management of commercial and maritime matters. It is highly necessary. Franklin is a wit and a humorist, I know. He may be a philosopher for all I know. But he is not a sufficient statesman for all the business he is in. He knows too little of American affairs, of the politics of Europe, and takes too little pains to inform himself of either to be sufficient for all those things—to be ambassador, secretary, admiral, consular agent, etc. Yet such is his name on both sides of the water, that it is best, perhaps, that he should be left there; but a secretary or consuls should be appointed to do the business or it will not be done, or if done, it will be by people who insinuate themselves into his confidence, without either such heads or hearts as Congress should trust. He is too old, too infirm, too indolent and dissipated, to be sufficient for the discharge of all the important duties of ambassador, board of war, board of treasury, commissary of prisoners, etc., as he is at present in that department, besides an immense correspondence and acquaintance, each of which would be enough for the whole time of the most active men in the vigor of youth.[1]

Vergennes's opinion of Franklin was more balanced, but he made some of the same criticisms in a letter to his minister in Philadelphia:

If you are asked our way of thinking in regard to Mr. Franklin, you will not hesitate to say that we esteem him as much for his patriotism as for the sagacity of his conduct and that it is in large part as a result of this sentiment and by the confidence that we put in the veracity of Mr. Franklin that I have determined to aid them in their financial embarrassment. . . . For the rest, although I esteem and respect Mr. Franklin, I am nonetheless obliged to agree that his age and his love for tranquility give him an apathy incompatible with the affairs with which he is charged and I see it with all the more pain as it is important matters on which I see this minister maintain silence whereas the good of the service requires he transmit his opinion to Congress.[2]

In spite of their differences, Adams and Vergennes agreed that Franklin's strength was his ability to inspire confidence, and his weakness was his

---

[1] Adams to Thomas McKean, 20 September 1779, Francis P. Wharton, ed., *The Revolutionary Diplomatic Correspondence of the United States*, 6 vols. (Washington Government Printing Office, 1889) 3: 332–33.

[2] Vergennes to Luzerne, 19 February 1781, Henri Doniol, ed., *Histoire de la participation de la France à l'établissement des États-Unis d'Amérique*, 5 vols, and supplement (Paris: Imprimerie Nationale, 1886–1898) 4: 583 (my translation). For a more positive appraisal stressing Franklin's zeal, patriotism, sagacity, and circumspection see Vergennes to Luzerne, 4 December 1780, ibid., p. 535.

indolence. This indolence, however, was a mixture of several elements. In part it was a question of health, although for most of the period Franklin spoke of his health as being good.[3] The problem was not debilitating disease, but rather an elderly man's need to save his physical and psychological resources for the matters he considered most pressing, such as negotiations with Vergennes or work on behalf of prisoners. Franklin's indolence was related to his hatred of controversy,[4] a weakness which led him to defer on occasion to his colleagues, as he did in August 1782. It is possible, though, that part of his seeming lack of effort was conscious choice. Two of Franklin's most astute biographers have pointed out the French aristocracy's desire not to appear vulgarly busy; Franklin was cultivating them by imitating their example (although he was far busier than he let them see).[5] I would add that Franklin may also have been putting up a brave front by not soliciting favors and by letting himself be courted.

One of the most unfortunate aspects of Franklin's lethargy was his failure to satisfy Congress's insatiable desire for news. Franklin confessed to his friend Lafayette, "You have found out by this time I am a very bad Correspondent. As I grow old I perceive my aversion to writing increases, and is become almost insurmountable."[6] Pressed by other correspondence, Franklin reduced his communications with Congress to essentials, depriving its members of the intelligence about French politics and military affairs they expected. There are some mitigating factors, however. First was the difficulty of finding safe conveyances for messages, given the fact merchant ship captains could not be trusted to dispose of dispatches when pursued by the British.[7] Moreover, Congress did not seem to grasp Franklin's message when his dispatches did get through. It took years of his begging before Congress appointed a consul to relieve Franklin of his mercantile responsibilities (and the first consul appointed was lost at sea). Worse still, Congress never did comprehend that the French goose could not lay golden eggs for American benefit forever.[8] Franklin confessed that the storm of bills to pay he received from Congress so terrified and vexed him that he was deprived of sleep "and so much indispos'd by continual anxiety, as to be render'd almost incapable of writing."[9] His failure to provide more military and naval intelligence was unavoidable because of the French government's distrust of American security, but given the time delays in-

---

[3] Franklin to his sister Jane Mecom, 5 October 1777 (APS); Franklin to William Carmichael, 31 March–7 April 1780 (DLC); Franklin to Jan Ingenhousz, Account of his medical case, 17 October 1777 (National-Bibliothek, Vienna); Franklin to Jan Ingenhousz, Journal of his health, 4 October 1778–16 January 1780 (DLC). For Franklin's medical problems see also Claude-Anne Lopez and Eugenia W. Herbert, *The Private Franklin: The Man and His Family* (New York: W. W. Norton and Company, 1975) p. 236.

[4] See in particular Franklin to Arthur Lee, 4 April 1778 (APS: a draft which probably was not sent).

[5] Lopez and Herbert, *The Private Franklin*, p. 237. The diligent and rather stodgy Vergennes is an exception which proves the rule.

[6] Franklin to Lafayette, 17 August 1779 (DLC).

[7] Franklin to Committee for Foreign Affairs, 26 May 1779 (DLC).

[8] For a particularly appalling example see Livingston to Franklin, 13 February 1782 (MH).

[9] Franklin to John Jay, 2 October 1780, Albert Henry Smyth, ed., *The Writings of Benjamin Franklin*, 10 vols. (New York: The Macmillan Company, 1907), 8: 142.

volved it probably would not have been worth running the risks of interception anyway.[10] Franklin's unwillingness to provide political intelligence may simply represent his very prudent decision not to become involved in French court politics.[11] Deane had courted disaster by criticizing the powerful comte de Maurepas and praising Vergennes's arch-enemy the duc de Choiseul,[12] and even Jay naively suggested publishing Necker's *Compte Rendu*, written as part of Necker's battle for power with Vergennes.[13] Franklin had the wisdom to deal with Vergennes and stay clear of Vergennes's rivals.[14] His best defense, however, exists in the dispatches he did send Congress: they are masterpieces of the art—succinct, straightforward, eloquent, tactful, and informative.

Of Franklin's other personal qualities, one which particularly seems to have struck his contemporaries was his circumspection. Vergennes first described Franklin as a person appearing intelligent but circumspect.[15] Adams as usual was less flattering: ". . . there is another, whose Love of Ease, and Dissipation, will prevent any thorough Reformation of any thing—and his Silence and Reserve, render it very difficult to do any Thing with him." Before "Silence" Adams first wrote and then crossed out the words "Cunning and."[16] Franklin himself in a piece called "The Morals of Chess" praised the game because it taught foresight, circumspection, and caution.[17]

The taciturn and prudent Franklin is maddening to historians.[18] It is far

---

[10] Instead of paraphrasing newspaper accounts Franklin preferred sending the newspapers themselves. Franklin to Livingston, 4 March 1782. Franklin also forwarded intelligence he received from unofficial sources but it was of poor quality. See List of Intelligence Reports, 12 January 1778–9 October 1780 (DNA). Franklin's one accomplishment was to send a warning that eleven British ships of the line were en route to intercept the French admiral d'Estaing. Samuel Cooper to Franklin, 1 July 1778 (APS); Jonathan R. Dull, *The French Navy and American Independence: A Study of Arms and Diplomacy, 1774–1787* (Princeton: Princeton University Press, 1975), pp. 112–24.

[11] See Franklin's Journal of Peace Negotiations, Carl Van Doren, *Benjamin Franklin's Autobiographical Writings* (New York: Viking Press, 1945), p. 577 for an example of Franklin's scruples.

[12] Charles Isham, ed., *The Deane Papers (Collections of the New-York Historical Society, 1887–1891)*, 1: 213.

[13] Jay to President of Congress, 22 March 1781, Wharton, *Revolutionary Diplomatic Correspondence*, 4: 322.

[14] Upon his arrival in France Franklin met Choiseul by accident, which prompted the British to hope he could be discredited. Edward Bancroft to Silas Deane, February 1777, *Deane Papers*, 2: 5–6. At the height of Necker's battle for power he and his wife invited Franklin to dinner; there is no record of whether he accepted. M. and Mme. Necker to Franklin, 21 March 1781 (APS).

[15] Vergennes to Aranda, 28 December 1776 (AHN).

[16] Diary entry of 9 February 1779. L. H. Butterfield, ed., *Diary and Autobiography of John Adams*, 4 vols. (Cambridge: The Belknap Press of Harvard University Press, 1961), 2: 346; for similar comments see John Adams to Sam Adams, 5 December 1778, *Collections of the Massachusetts Historical Society* 73(1925): 74; extract from the *Boston Patriot*, 15 May 1811, Charles Francis Adams, ed., *The Works of John Adams, Second President of the United States, with a Life of the Author*, 10 vols. (Boston: Little, Brown and Company, 1856), 1: 661.

[17] This piece was written no later than 1779 but first appeared in *The Columbian Magazine* 1(1786): 159–61.

[18] See Gerald Stourzh's comment, *Benjamin Franklin and American Foreign Policy*, 2d ed. (Chicago: University of Chicago Press, 1969), p. xiii; see also Julian P. Boyd, ed., *The Papers of Thomas Jefferson*, 19 vols. to date (Princeton: Princeton University Press, 1950–), 8: 262.

easier to study a John Adams, who reveals between the lines the feelings and motives he does not state directly. Franklin's silence and reserve were among his prime assets as a diplomat, however. By his silence, or at most an enigmatic phrase, the diplomat can keep his motives hidden while avoiding the faux pas of a direct lie, which not only is bad form but undermines credibility. One of Franklin's major objections to the use of multiple commissioners was the difficulty of their maintaining secrecy as to their motives.[19] He was able to keep his innermost feelings masked in both the negotiations of 1777 and of 1782; like Washington, Jefferson, and Madison, he earned his contemporaries' respect by measuring his words.

Franklin's caution, prudence, and common sense paid off in his winning and keeping the confidence of the French government. No blustering Adams or hostile Jay, Franklin's politeness could mask a threat, cover a change of policy, or create a desired impression, while always leaving him a line of retreat. Such skill was not something that could be learned from books. Adams studied diligently and could not have been less suited to life at the French court; Franklin apparently did not bother.[20] Except for brief experiments, there were no training schools for diplomats in the eighteenth century.[21] French diplomats were often sent to important posts at a very early age and after very limited prior experience[22]; like them, Franklin learned by doing.

Franklin did differ from European diplomats in several ways. First, European diplomats almost always came from a social class which could be expected to inculcate a poise and self-confidence not to be found in the fifteenth child of an immigrant tallow-chandler and soap maker. (Although not a formal diplomatic post, Franklin's service in London certainly played a key part in his acquiring this polish.) Second, Franklin was markedly older than his diplomatic colleagues, both European and American. Most important, unlike a European diplomat, Franklin had to function without guidance. The difficulty of communications was only part of this. Gérard and Luzerne in Philadelphia may have heard infrequently from the French court, but they did receive guidance from a foreign minister with a lifetime of experience and a coherent foreign policy. The Committees of Secret Correspondence and of Foreign Affairs provided Franklin with only difficulties; Livingston, the secretary for foreign affairs who took over their responsibilities in October 1781, was a 34-year-old diplomatic neophyte.[23]

---

[19] Franklin to Lovell, 22 July 1778 (DNA).

[20] Butterfield, *Adams Diary and Autobiography*, 4: 145–47; Franklin to the chevalier de Champigny, 24 July 1778 (APS); Benjamin Rush to John Adams, 31 October 1807, L. H. Butterfield, ed., *Letters of Benjamin Rush*, 2 vols. (Princeton: Princeton University Press, 1951), 2: 953.

[21] For the lack of training for diplomats see William James Roosen, *The Age of Louis XIV: The Rise of Modern Diplomacy* (Cambridge, Mass.: Schenkman Publishers, 1976). pp. 74–77; David Boyne Horn, *The British Diplomatic Service, 1689–1789* (Oxford: Clarendon Press, 1961), pp. 96–99, 109, 136–40.

[22] Examples include the marquis de Vérac (b. 1743) sent to Copenhagen in 1776 and St. Petersburg in 1780, the comte de Montmorin (b. 1745) sent to Madrid in 1777, the duc de La Vauguyon (b. 1746) sent to The Hague in 1776, the chevalier de La Luzerne (b. 1741) sent to Philadelphia in 1779 and the marquis de Noailles (b. 1743) sent to London in 1776.

[23] For contrasting views of Livingston's abilities compare William C. Stinchcombe, *The*

Franklin had to teach himself and function without guidance; his success can be measured by comparing his mistakes in early 1777 to his sure hand in the peace negotiations.

A final word of caution is necessary before we leave Franklin the diplomat. One can legitimately compare his aptitude to that of Congress's other diplomats, but it is possible to overemphasize the effectiveness of his negotiating style. One of the most elementary of negotiating techniques, also often used in interrogation, is that of having as a team someone harsh and demanding and someone reasonable and conciliatory. After exposing the other party to threats and intimidation it is often possible to extract concessions or confessions by an appearance of sympathy and reasonableness. Franklin had the good fortune to be linked with some of the most obnoxious and unreasonable negotiators with whom Vergennes ever had to deal. Franklin's sweet reasonableness and tact derived some of their effectiveness from their contrast with the bluster and gaucheries of Silas Deane, Arthur Lee, John Adams, and John Laurens.[24] An emphasis on etiquette of course can be a way of masking a brutal and amoral underlying reality; eighteenth-century European international relations were as violent as the courtly and murderous world of the fifteenth century.[25] Nevertheless, it is easy to shudder along with the exquisitely courteous Vergennes at the terrible Americans and to suspect he may have been so accommodating to Franklin partly so as not to have to deal with Franklin's colleagues.[26] Franklin had far less luck with the British, who had no illusions that he would be more conciliatory than any other American.

What then do we learn from Franklin the diplomat about Franklin the man? What has most impressed me is the degree to which even Franklin the diplomat was a man of feeling. His shrewdness and prudence broke down completely when friends like Bancroft and Carmichael were in-

American Revolution and the French Alliance (Syracuse: Syracuse University Press, 1969), p. 192 and George Dangerfield, *Chancellor Robert R. Livingston of New York, 1746–1813* (New York: Harcourt, Brace and Company, 1960), p. 146. The lack of even a rudimentary bureaucracy is demonstrated by the fact that not until 24 November 1781 were dispatches to Franklin numbered and Franklin asked to do the same, Livingston to Franklin of that date (DNA). Let us not forget that the United States was a developing country in which experienced diplomats, like seasoned admirals and generals, were not to be expected. See Robert A. East, *Business Enterprise in the American Revolutionary Era* (New York: Columbia University Press, 1938), pp. 13–29.

[24] There are tantalizing hints Franklin may have played the game deliberately. See Isham, *Deane Papers*, 5: 438–40; Franklin to Jay, 12 April 1781 (DLC).

[25] Compare two of the greatest masterpieces of historical literature: Albert Sorel, *Europe and the French Revolution: The Political Traditions of the Old Régime*, trans. Alfred Cobban and J. W. Hunt (Garden City, New York: Anchor Books, 1971), originally published 1885; Johan Huizinga, *The Waning of the Middle Ages: A Study of the Forms of Life, Thought and Art in France and the Netherlands in the XIVth and XVth Centuries*, trans. F. Hopman (Garden City, New York: Anchor Books, 1949), originally published 1924.

[26] Vergennes did stress to his ministers in Philadelphia the fear that anyone replacing Franklin would be worse, Henri Doniol, ed., *Histoire de la participation de la France à l'établissement des États-Unis d'Amérique*, 5 vols. and supplement (Paris: Imprimerie Nationale, 1886–1898) 4: 583–84.

volved, and he became a victim of his tendency to believe the best of others.[27] (This may even have been a factor in one of Franklin's few negotiating mistakes, that of taking the risk Shelburne's intentions were good, and therefore sending him the proposal to cede Canada in the interests of reconciliation.) Franklin's reserve and secrecy led others often to see him as vain, ambitious, vengeful, self-righteous, and unscrupulous. Such accusations are not devoid of truth, but they do not do justice to his other qualities. The majority of those who knew him saw Franklin as a man of benevolence, good will, and decency. He had a difficult time refusing favors to others, whether money or letters of introduction, and he was repeatedly defrauded.[28] His tendency to listen to his heart was a failing in Franklin the diplomat, but it makes him a more sympathetic person than the icy Franklin of myth.

Franklin's heart may also have been the source of his extraordinary strength. For a man of his passion self-control must not have come easily, yet in spite of any inner doubts or fears he was able for five difficult years to preserve unshaken an image of equanimity and confidence. Under the terrible challenges of 1777 and 1782 he did not crack as did Deane and Jay. Certainly his confidence in America was genuine; Adams, in discussing the possibilities of obtaining a loan in the Netherlands, paid tribute to Franklin's innate optimism in admitting "I have not one grain of your faith nor hope."[29] Nevertheless, I believe we must look elsewhere to find the source of this frail old man's toughness and energy. Franklin had loved both Britain and America, indeed had viewed them as part of a whole, the British Empire.[30] This object of his love had been torn apart and now the British were burning American cities, assaulting American liberties, killing Franklin's fellow Americans. I believe the wellsprings from which Franklin drew were his love for America and his hurt, bitterness, and anger at Britain.

Americans today seem to have an impression of Franklin as less "revolutionary" than a Sam Adams or John Adams. Franklin's moderation, hatred of war, cosmopolitanism, and playfulness appeal to many of us as much as they distressed many of Franklin's contemporaries. Some of these contemporaries also disagreed with Franklin's tactics or distrusted his membership in the Walpole Company and his use of a Loyalist's son as his secretary.[31] Most of the revolutionaries who knew Franklin, however, regarded him as one of their own.[32] He shared their faith in American

---

[27] This was a long-standing attitude of Franklin's. For his belief that political leadership consisted of drawing out others' inherent good intentions see William S. Hanna, *Benjamin Franklin and Pennsylvania Politics* (Stanford: Stanford University Press, 1964), p. 111.

[28] For an example of Franklin's tenderheartedness see Franklin to Mrs. R. Parson, ca. 15 August 1778 (APS), sending a guinea to the wife of a man who had defrauded him of fifteen.

[29] Adams to Franklin, 16 April 1781, Charles Frances Adams, *Works of John Adams*, 7: 389.

[30] Franklin to David Hartley, 3 September 1778 (DLC).

[31] Madison's notes of the congressional debate of 30 December 1782, Worthington Chauncey Ford et al., eds., *Journals of the Continental Congress, 1774–1789*, 35 vols. (Washington: Library of Congress and National Archives, 1904–1976), 23: 873.

[32] Even John Adams; see Butterfield, *Adams Diary and Autobiography*, 4: 41–42. Pauline Maier points out that the Loyalists frequently mentioned Franklin as the American arch-conspirator,

triumph, their contempt for Britain, their self-righteous belief in their cause (which he claimed Europe saw as "the Cause of all Mankind").[33] For all of his hatred of war, he could urge the burning or plundering of Liverpool or Glasgow in retaliation for what the British had done to America.[34] We have lost the emotional content that the burning of a Charlestown or Falmouth or the British use of Indians or the hiring of Hessians had for Franklin and his fellow Americans.[35] For Franklin the bitterness was compounded by the fact that the British had taken from him his son William, whose Loyalism he never forgave.[36]   Perhaps what makes it hardest for us to understand not only Franklin but the entire revolutionary generation is our cynicism about public life. Franklin was a public man to a degree we now find difficult to appreciate. Adams said of him, "He has a Passion for Reputation and Fame, as strong as you can imagine, and his Time and Thoughts are chiefly employed to obtain it . . ."[37] This hunger to be recognized for one's public excellence by one's fellows has motivated politicians ever since the Greek city-state, and Franklin's generation was far closer to that world than we are.[38] Not only were they products of classical culture but they, like the Greeks, were part of a political system predating modern political parties. Political issues certainly did exist in colonial politics, but still politics remained an arena in which one could demonstrate one's right to the honor of selection by one's fellows. Such electors did not have the benefit of voting records compiled by ideological or interest groups, and party labels were premature or nonexistent. The politician thus was more dependent then than now on his reputation among his peers. Since 1800 classical culture has lost its meaning, and we have seen the rise of political parties and issue-oriented candidates. However inevitable the changes, one of their by-products has been the debasement of politics. No

---

Pauline Maier, *The Old Revolutionaries: Political Lives in the Age of Samuel Adams* (New York: Alfred A. Knopf, 1980), pp. 8–9.

[33] Franklin to Samuel Cooper, 1 May 1777, Smyth, *Writings of Franklin*, 7: 56. See also Franklin to Cooper, 27 October 1779, ibid. pp. 407–9. With his repeated criticisms of American luxury Franklin was also closer to his Boston origins than we are prone to think.

[34] American Commissioners to Committee for Foreign Affairs, 25 May 1777 (DNA); Franklin to John Paul Jones, 28 April 1779 (DNA); Franklin to James Lovell, 17 October 1779 (DNA). Franklin did order Jones not to burn any cities unless reasonable ransom was refused and notice to evacuate was given the sick, aged, women, and children.

[35] Franklin in his bitterness was prone to believe the worst of the British. See Franklin to Jan Ingenhousz, 12 February–6 March 1777 (CtY); Franklin's "Supplement to the Boston Independent Chronicle," ca. 12 March 1782 (CtY); Franklin to John Adams, 22 April 1782 (MHi). For Franklin's personal animosity toward George III, see Butterfield, *Adams Diary and Autobiography*, 4: 150.

[36] See Lopez and Herbert, *The Private Franklin*, passim, for Franklin's closeness to William.

[37] Diary entry of 10 May 1779, Butterfield, *Adams Diary and Autobiography*, 2: 367.

[38] Compare Henry Steele Commager, *The Empire of Reason: How Europe Imagined and America Realized the Enlightenment* (Garden City, New York: Anchor Press/Doubleday, 1977), pp. 126–31; Douglass Adair, "Fame and the Founding Fathers," in Trevor Colbourn, ed., *Fame and the Founding Fathers: Essays by Douglass Adair* (New York: W. W. Norton and Company, 1974), pp. 4–26; Stanley Idzerda, "Character as Destiny: A New Look at Lafayette's Career," in *La France et l'esprit de '76* (Clermont-Ferrand: Faculté des lettres et sciences humaines de l'Université de Clermont-Ferrand II, 1978), pp. 79–94; Paul W. Conner, *Poor Richard's Politicks: Benjamin Franklin and The New American Order* (New York: Oxford University Press, 1966) pp. 29, 179–95.

longer do we see the political arena as the testing ground of personal excellence.[39] In this estrangement from politics we find ourselves distanced from the founding fathers and their values. In neglecting Franklin's diplomacy in our concentration on the other aspects of his life, we distort the historical record. Franklin the diplomat is one of the supreme accomplishments by which Franklin the man deserves to be measured.

---

[39] This is not to deny the benefits in status, business contacts, etc., conferred by eighteenth century political life. See Jack N. Rakove, *The Beginnings of National Politics: An Interpretive History of the Continental Congress* (New York: Alfred A. Knopf, 1979), pp. 7, 223, 232, 261.

INDEX

Adams, John: on Franklin's qualifications, activities, 4, 27, 45, 65, 67, 70, 71; in Netherlands, 4, 15, 26–27, 47, 49, 56; as radical, 7; and Vergennes, 7n, 47, 62; views of, on naval affairs, 9, 51; reluctance of, to ask for foreign aid, 12; Franklin advises, 15; Francophobia of, 16; replaces Deane as commissioner, 33, 44–45; as peace commissioner, 47, 55–56, 59, 61n, 62; Franklin's opinion of, 47; ease of discerning motives of, 68

Adams, Samuel, 70

Affaires de l'Angleterre et de l'Amérique, 17n, 26, 34

Alliance, Treaty of, 8, 11, 13, 20, 29–35

America: Franklin's concern for growth, security of, 2, 9; importance of, to British Empire, 2, 10; Franklin spokesman in England for, 3, 12; Vergennes desires independence of, 10, 47, 63; French financial aid to, 11, 14, 22, 28–29, 48–50, 56, 61, 65; dependence of, 12–13, 49–51, 56; Spanish financial aid to, 14–15; Franklin's optimism about, 15–16; military weakness of, 42n; devaluates currency, 47; news of armistice arrives in, 64; as developing country, 69n

Amity and Commerce, Treaty of, 8, 11, 13, 14, 15n, 30–32, 44

Amsterdam, 12, 20, 37, 46, 48

Aranda, the conde de, 14, 28, 61

Army, Continental, 5, 8–9, 19, 21, 36, 48, 63

Army, French, 50–51, 56

Austin, Jonathan Loring, 29, 43–44

Austria, 9, 31n, 47, 62n

Bache, Benjamin Franklin, 1, 16, 42

Bancroft, Edward, 33–38, 40, 69

Barclay, Thomas, 48

Barney, Joshua, 61

Beaumarchais, P.-A. Caron de, 29n, 36n, 37

"Benson," 33–35

Benson, Peter, Paul, and James, 35n

Berlin, 15, 21, 37, 46

Bingham, William, 39

Bordeaux, 21, 35n

Boux, Jacques, 19–20, 48

Burgoyne, John, 27, 29

Cabinet, British. *See* government, British

Camden, C. Pratt, Lord, 43

Canada, 5, 6, 13, 30n, 54–55, 63n

Carmichael, William, 24, 26n, 37–40, 42, 56, 69

Castries, the duc de, 45

Catherine II, empress of Russia, 4

Charles III, king of Spain, 21, 61

Chatham, William Pitt, Lord, 43–44

Chaumont, J.-D. Le Ray de, 33

Chess, 67

Choiseul, the duc de, 67

Commerce. *See* trade

Commissioners: proposal to send to various courts, 21

Commissioners, Indian, 5

Commissioners in France, American: 13, 15n, 31, 14, 16, 22–25, 16, 19, 20, 21, 22, 28, 22–25, 23, 23, 25, 26, 27, 28, 28, 28, 28–29, 29, 29n, 37–39, 38, 40, 40–41, 43–44, 45; pledges of, 16; and frigates, 19–20; dissention among, 25–27, 44–45; negotiations of, 29–32

Commissioners, peace, 47, 54–64

Commission seekers, 19

Commissions, naval, 22

Committee for Foreign Affairs, 15n, 26n

Committee of Secret Correspondence, 6, 12, 13n, 15n, 22, 25, 37

Compte Rendu, 67

Constitution (frigate), 20

Consuls, American, 8, 48, 66

Continental Congress: Franklin serves in, 5–8, 12–13, 15, 17; establishes mission in France, 5, 6, 13; instructions from, 7, 13, 15n, 16, 22, 31, 54, 60, 63; recalls Deane, 19, 44; Deane's suggestions to, 21–22, 36; selects commissioners to various courts, 21; authorizes hostilities against Portugal, 21; left final decision on export duty article, 32; fails to appoint professional diplomatic staff in France, 42; elects Franklin minister plenipotentiary, 45; draws bills of exchange on European diplomatic representatives, 45n, 49, 66; French lobby against Adams in, 47, 62; selects peace commissioners, 47, 49

Conyngham, Gustavus, 24, 33, 37–40

Copenhagen, 68n

Council of state, French. *See* court and government, French

Court, British: Franklin draws lessons from, 4–5

Court and government, French: difficulties of negotiating with, 2; gives financial aid to America, 11, 14, 22, 28–29, 48–50, 56, 61, 65; and relations with Great Britain, 14, 22–25, 27, 29–31, 43–44, 60; Franklin's view of, 16; dealings of, with Spain, 17n, 29, 30, 43–44, 51, 61n, 62–63, 65; commissioners attempt to procure loan from, 22, 28; policy of, toward prizes, privateers, 22–25, 27; formally recognizes American commissioners, 43–44; Franklin accredited to, 45–46; Franklin turns British correspondence over to, 53–54, 57n; peace negotiations of, 58–63

Dana, Francis, 15, 49

Deane, Silas: mission to France of (1776), 6, 13n, 19–22; appointed commissioner, 6, 14; Francophobia of, 16; describes Franklin's diplomatic approach, 16–17; recalled by Congress, 19, 44; and procurement of military supplies, 20; suggestions to Congress by, 21–22, 36; dispute between A. Lee and, 25–26; opposes export duties, 31–32; dealings of, with Bancroft, 33–36; as stockjobber, 35–36; congressional treatment of, 36, 40; Franklin breaks with, 36; and Beaumarchais, 36n, 37; and Carmichael, 37–40; attempts to establish cartel, 37; Carmichael's testimony against, 40

Deane, Simeon, 40

Declaration of Independence, 5, 6

De Kalb, Gen. J., 19

D'Estaing, Admiral C.-H., comte, 67n

Du Coudray, P.-C.-J.-B. Tronson, 19

Dumas, C. G. F., 6n, 12, 26

Du Mauroy, C.-L., vicomte, 19

Dunkirk, 23–24, 39

Duportail, Louis Lebègue de Presle, 19

Eden, William, 33–34, 35n

Edinburgh, University of, 37

"Edwards," 34–35

England: Franklin in, 2–5, 11; Rayneval's mission to, 62

Export duties, 31–32

Farmers General, 19, 22

Florence, 21, 45–46

Florida, 13, 31, 54, 59, 63–64

Fox, Charles James, 54–57

Ford, Hezekiah, 40

France: position of, in European balance of power, 9–10; Franklin describes people of, 16n; use of ports of, 22–25, 27, 39; Franklin influences public opinion in, 26–27; rearmament of, 30, 32; as "husband" of America, 49n; needs peace, 62–63

"François," 34

Franklin, Benjamin: religious views of, vi, 3n, 43; as politician, vi, 1–2, 5–8, 11–13, 70–72; diverse careers of, 1; character of, 1–2, 5, 7, 11, 41–42, 53, 65–71; writings of, 1, 3, 5, 26, 67; as a scientist, 1, 2, 11, 57; as a colonial agent, 1–5, 11, 68; 2, 9; feelings of, toward Great Britain, 2–4, 11, 27, 28, 41, 53, 70–71; uses lobbying tactics, 2–3, 5, 8, 11, 41; parliamentary contacts of, 3, 43–44, 54; pursues royal government, 3, 11; in Stamp Act crisis, 3; leaks Hutchinson letters, 3, 4n

Negotiates with members of Cabinet, 4, 11–12; and George III, 4, 53, 71n; congressional service of, 5–8, 12–13, 15, 17; as American postmaster general, 5, 41; various appointments of (1775–1776), 5, 6; helps draft Declaration of Independence, 5, 6; military background of, 5, 6, 8–9; selected as commissioner to France, 5, 6, 13; describes to A. Lee his life as congressman, 5; obedience of, to congressional instructions, 7, 50–51, 54, 60, 63

Background in economics of, 8; as free trade advocate, 8, 46n; uses Lafayette, 9, 50–51; ignorance of law, statecraft by, 9, 65, 68; procures funds from French government, 11, 48–50, 61; in peace negotiations, 11, 41, 53–64, 70; as "courted virgin," 11, 15, 17, 49, 66; as early supporter of independence, 12; on need for foreign assistance, 12–13, 28–29, 30n; on use of threats, 13; opposes begging for help, 15, 29, 51; adopts policy of reserve, 16–17, 28; on French court, 16; on French people, 16n; is selected commissioner to Spain, 21

Enemies of, 21; admits imprudence of using Dunkirk, 24; influences French public opinion, 26–27; social activities of, 27, 42, 46; and negotiations with North government, 27n, 29–30, 43, 53; discusses federal union with Great Britain, 27n, 30n, 57; continued optimism of, 28–29, 51, 70; in negotiations for alliance, commercial treaty, 29–31; opposes export duties, 31–32; disorderliness, inattention to security of, 33, 40–42, 65; and Bancroft, 33–34, 40, 69; breaks with Deane, 36; and Carmichael, 40, 42, 69; concern for American prisoners by, 40, 46, 54, 61, 66; feelings about America, 41, 53, 65, 70; self-discipline required by, 42; on evils of war, 42

Makes final attempt to avert war, 43–44; and Shelburne, 44, 53–60; named minister plenipotentiary, 45; describes Adams, 47; named peace commissioner, 47; tenders resignation, 48–49; relations of, with Adams, Jay, 49; suggests Great Britain cede Canada, 54; concern for Vergennes's feelings, 56n, 59–61; health of, 58–59, 65–66; and Loyalists, 60, 71; on possible continuation of war, 64; differs from European diplomats, 68–69; as man of feeling, 69–70; as revolutionary, 70–71

Franklin, Deborah (wife of B. Franklin), 2n, 49–50

Franklin, William, 60n, 71

Franklin, William Temple, 1, 38, 41, 42, 45, 61, 70

Gabriel Antonio de Bourbon, don, 21

Gates, Horatio, 7

Gazette de Leide, 26n
Genet, Édme-Jacques, 34
George III, 4, 33–35, 53, 55n, 59, 71n
Gérard, Conrad-Alexandre, 14, 29–31, 45, 47n, 50, 68
Gibbes, Sir Philip, 27n, 30n
Government, British: Franklin negotiates with, 4; Franklin's proposal to (1776), 13–14; Franklin's terms for peace with (1777), 27n; and prisoner relief negotiations, 43–44; peace commissioners named to deal with, 47; sends representative to Franklin (1782), 53; in peace negotiations, 54–64
Government, royal, 3, 11
Great Britain: Franklin's feelings toward, 2–4, 11, 27, 28, 41, 53, 70–71; Vergennes wishes to weaken, 9–10; Franklin's posture toward (1775–1776), 12; relations with France, 14, 22–25, 27, 29–31, 43–44, 60; and the Netherlands, 20, 46; Franklin discusses possibility of American federal union with, 30n, 57; Fox proposes to ally with Prussia, Russia, 57; encouraged to attack Florida, 59, 64; public opinion in, 61, 63
Grenville, Thomas, 55–56

Hague, The, 15n, 47, 68n
Harris, Sir James, 4
Hartley, David, 43, 53
Hodgson, William, 61
Holland. *See* Netherlands, the
Hood, Sir Samuel, 59n
Hortalez, Roderigue and Company, 37
Howe, Richard, 5, 6, 12
Hutchinson letters, 3, 4n
Hynson, Joseph, 37n, 38

Ingenhousz, Jan, 57
"Intended Vindication and Offer," 6, 26n
Izard, Ralph, 21, 31, 45–46

Jay, John, 7, 15, 16, 40, 47, 49, 54–56, 58–64, 67–69
Jeans, Thomas, 38
Jefferson, Thomas, 4–5, 36, 47, 68
Joly de Fleury, J.-F., 45

Keppel, A., viscount, 59n

Lafayette, the marquis de, 9, 19, 50–51, 66
La Rochefoucauld, the duc de, 26
Laurens, Henry, 13, 47, 49, 56, 59
Laurens, John, 48–49, 69
La Vauguyon, the duc de, 68n
Lee, Arthur: appointed commissioner, 6, 14; activities in London of, 6n, 37; dispatches of, 9; mission to Spain, 14, 21; mission to Berlin, 15; Franklin's advice to, 15; Francophobia of, 16; selected commissioner to Spain, 21; dispute between Deane and, 25–

26, 40n; relays R. H. Lee's warnings, 28; agrees with Franklin to issue no ultimatums, 29; demands change in commercial treaty, 31–32; dispatches Carmichael with letter, 37; Carmichael testifies against, 40; discredited with French, 40, 44; Thornton, Ford secretaries of, 40, 43–44; and Shelburne, 44
Lee, Charles, 7
Lee, Richard Henry, 21, 28
Lee, William, 21, 25–26, 36n, 45–46
Livingston, Captain M., 34–35
Livingston, Robert R., 55, 68
London: Franklin in, 1, 2n, 68; A. Lee in, 37; French ambassador in, 43–44, 68n; H. Laurens in, 49
London Public Advertiser, 26
Louis XVI, king of France, 30, 44, 49n, 56
Loyalists, 54, 55, 60, 70n, 71
"Lupton, George," 33
Luzerne, the chevalier de La, 47, 48, 65, 68

Madison, James, 64n, 68
Madrid, 21, 68n
Massachusetts, 3, 8, 29
Maurepas, the comte de, 63
Montbarey, the prince de, 45
Montmorin, the comte de, 51, 68n
Morris, Robert, 7, 12, 25, 42n
Morris, Thomas, 25
"Moses," 34n
Munitions and military supplies, 13–14, 20, 28, 29n, 37, 46, 48, 64

Nantes, 20, 37, 41
Navy, British, 25, 59, 67n
Navy, French, 23, 25, 50, 62
Navy, Spanish, 23, 64
Necker, Jacques, 45, 67
Netherlands, the: Adams in, 4, 15, 26–27, 47, 49, 56; frigates to be built in, 19–20; and Great Britain, 20, 46; newspaper items published in, 26; Franklin's proposed mission to, 45; funds raised in, 47, 48
Newfoundland, 16, 25, 31, 63
Newspapers, Franklin's writings for, 3, 5, 26, 67n
New York, 56, 59, 64
Nicholson, Captain S., 37n
Noailles, the marquis de, 23, 68n
North, F., "Lord," 27n, 33

Oswald, Richard, 54–58

Paine, Thomas, 13n, 28
Paris, 14, 21, 28, 37, 48
Parliament, 3, 28, 43, 59–60
Penn, Richard and Thomas, 1–2, 11
Pennsylvania, 1–3, 5–6, 7n, 8, 11, 26n
Prisoners, American, 9, 26n, 40, 43, 46, 49, 54, 61, 66

Privy Council, 3, 11
Prizes, 22–25, 27, 39, 46
Pulaski, C., 19
Pulteney, William, 53

Quakers, 4

Rayneval, Joseph-Mathis Gérard de, 56, 62, 63n
Reprisal (brig), 22, 25
"Resolution on Trade," 6
Rhode Island, 50
Rockingham, C. W.-W., Lord, 54, 57
Russia, 9, 15, 47, 57, 62n

St. Petersburg, 4, 15, 49, 68n
"St. Pierre," 34n
Saratoga, Battle of, 29, 40
Sartine, A.-R.-J.-G.-G. de, 45
Secret Committee, 6, 8, 12, 25
Secret service, British, 23, 33–40
Ségur, the marquis de, 45
Shelburne, W. P. Fitzmaurice, Lord, 44, 53–60
Smith, Lt. Col. Edward, 38
South Carolina (frigate), 48
Spain: American relations with, 14, 16, 59, 64; A. Lee's mission to, 14–15; Jay's mission to, 15, 37, 40, 47, 49, 56; French dealings with, 17n, 29, 30, 43–44, 51, 61n, 62–63; Franklin named commissioner to, 21; war aims of, 31, 63; Franklin's suspicions of, 55n; in peace negotiations, 60–64
Stamp Act, 3
Stock market, London, 34–36
Stormont, D. Murray, Lord, 25, 28, 38–39
"Supplement to the Boston Independent Chronicle," 26

Thornton, John, 40, 43, 44n
Tobacco, 19
Trade, 10, 14, 16
Turgot, A.-R.-J., 27
Turks, 62n

Uniforms, 20
United States. *See* America
Utrecht, Treaty of, 23n

Van Zandt, James, 33–34, 38–39
Vardill, Rev. John, 37n
Vaughan, Benjamin, 57n, 58n
Vérac, the marquis de, 68n
Vergennes, Charles Gravier, comte de: distrusts Adams, 7n; desires American independence, 10, 47, 63; responds to Franklin's appeals, 10; and American commissioners, 14, 22–25; refuses open aid to America, 14; policy of, on prizes, 22–25; proposes idea of convoy for American warships, 24; prepares France for war, 27; warns commissioners about security breach, 28; promises loan, 28–29; and Beaumarchais's goods, 29n; in negotiations for alliance, commercial treaty, 29–31; approves Carmichael's secret meetings, 38; and Austro-Russian mediation proposal, 47; advises against Dana mission, 49; authorizes separate American peace negotiations, 56; opinion of, about British Navy, 59n; motives of, during peace negotiations, 62–63; appraises Franklin, 65, 67
Versailles, 44, 61
Vienna, 21, 45, 46
Von Steuben, F. W. A., 19

Walpole, Thomas, 34n, 35, 43
Walpole Company, 34n, 35
War of 1812, 60
Washington, George, 7, 19, 36, 48, 51, 68
Washington (packet), 61
Wentworth, Paul, 29–30, 38
West, American, 41, 55, 62–64
West Indies, 14, 16, 64
Wharton, Samuel, 34–35
Wickes, Lambert, 22–25, 40n
Williams, Jonathan, Jr., 25–26, 41, 61

Yorktown, Battle of, 50–51

PUBLICATIONS

OF

The American Philosophical Society

The publications of the American Philosophical Society consist of PROCEEDINGS, TRANSACTIONS, MEMOIRS, and YEAR BOOK.

THE PROCEEDINGS contains papers which have been read before the Society in addition to other papers which have been accepted for publication by the Committee on Publications. In accordance with the present policy one volume is issued each year, consisting of six bimonthly numbers, and the price is $20.00 net per volume.

THE TRANSACTIONS, the oldest scholarly journal in America, was started in 1769. In accordance with the present policy each annual volume is a collection of monographs, each issued as a part. The current annual subscription price is $50.00 net per volume. Individual copies of the TRANSACTIONS are offered for sale.

Each volume of the MEMOIRS is published as a book. The titles cover the various fields of learning; most of the recent volumes have been historical. The price of each volume is determined by its size and character, but subscribers are offered a 20 percent discount.

The YEAR BOOK is of considerable interest to scholars because of the reports on grants for research and to libraries for this reason and because of the section dealing with the acquisitions of the Library. In addition it contains the Charter and Laws, and lists of members, and reports of committees and meetings. The YEAR BOOK is published about April 1 for the preceding calendar year. The current price is $5.00.

An author desiring to submit a manuscript for publication should send it to the Editor, American Philosophical Society, 104 South Fifth Street, Philadelphia, Pa. 19106.

www.ingramcontent.com/pod-product-compliance
Lightning Source LLC
Chambersburg PA
CBHW061756260326
41914CB00006B/1127